Synthesis Lectures on Human-Centered Informatics

Series Editor

John M. Carroll, College of Information Sciences and Technology, Penn State University, University Park, PA, USA

This series publishes short books on Human-Centered Informatics (HCI), at the inter-section of the cultural, the social, the cognitive, and the aesthetic with computing and information technology. Lectures encompass a huge range of issues, theories, technolo-gies, designs, tools, environments, and human experiences in knowledge, work, recreation, and leisure activity, teaching and learning, etc. The series publishes state-of-the-art syn-theses, case studies, and tutorials in key areas. It shares the focus of leading international conferences in HCI.

John Long

Guide to Framing Design Practice for UX

 Springer

John Long
University College London
London, UK

ISSN 1946-7680   ISSN 1946-7699 (electronic)
Synthesis Lectures on Human-Centered Informatics
ISBN 978-3-031-68980-2   ISBN 978-3-031-68981-9 (eBook)
https://doi.org/10.1007/978-3-031-68981-9

This Springer imprint is published by the registered company Springer Nature Switzerland AG
The registered company address is: Gewerbestrasse 11, 6330 Cham, Switzerland

If disposing of this product, please recycle the paper.

To Doris, also to Hadley, Ben and their families.
To Paola for listening… and listening…
To JM and PB—mentors, protagonists and friends.

Preface

Welcome to the World of User Experience (UX)

'The topic of UX is complex and struggles with definition, scope, and perceived utility. At the same time, everyone wants it, feels it's important and yet no-one completely owns it. Experience is unique; mine is mine and yours is yours and yet design would get quite complicated without some commonality, a set of norms, rules of thumb or good old-fashioned principles'.

—Seb Chakraborty (2023)

'I love design, data, making things and then making them better. I'm lucky that I do UX. I love the simplicity of the idea at its core—test and iterate.

*   I've been doing this for the past 20 years for more organisations than you can shake a stick at.....Everywhere I have been, as a Head of UX, I have set up a lab. This is the easiest and most effective way to get a design mindset into an organisation and build client trust in a solution. And the most creative part of the design process happens when you put users in front of a product. The friction between the product and the user is where novel solutions emerge. I nurture talent and build teams of skilled and dedicated UXers that have fun and produce great work. I provide them with space and time to think by Uxing UX, creating tools and processes to raise standards and save time'.*

—James Sinclair (2023)

UX is alive and kicking—as witnessed by the above comments. Despite this, at this time it is not easy to understand or to engage with UX. It is not yet well formed. There is little consensus as to what it is about, what it does, how it does it and what effect it has. UX takes many forms. Hence, the need for a guide to help people find their way around and so to better engage with it. This is true for both UX practitioners and UX researchers. In particular, between the design knowledge the latter are trying to acquire and the attempts of the former to apply it.

UX formation is little in evidence. Neither does it appear feasible at this time by fiat. That is by top-down, formal and framework-driven approaches. In contrast, this guide takes a bottom-up, informal and practice-driven approach. However, it offers no panacea for the problem of UX formation itself. Its approach merely constitutes one possible prerequisite. In addition, the book opens up ways forward for UX and the identification of remaining issues.

About This Book

The title *Guide to Framing Design Practice for UX* establishes the goals of this book. Its general scope is UX, and its general aim is to help readers better engage with UX design practice. Together, scope and content characterise UX as a movement, whose members are developing shared ideas to specify and to implement UX. The specific scope of the book is operationalised as framing UX design practice. The specific content comprises a guide to framing such practice. The core of the book is the analysis of the conduct and reporting of framing UX design practice as contributed by experienced UX practitioners. Conduct includes types of UX design practice and the structures supporting them, and report includes relevant case studies.

However, the book also opens up novel ways of moving UX forward. The guide, thus, contributes to UX formation of both practice and research, if only in the longer term. The practice is that of UX designers, the research that of UX researchers, the experience is that of interactive technology users/customers/humans as individuals and as organisations. Framing is how practitioners conduct and report their UX design practice.

About the Author

I feel qualified to write such a guidebook only on the basis of, and thanks to, source materials contributed by onetime students and now experienced UX practitioners. As concerns my other major publications, I have published one book in 2021, co-authored three more (with Lim in 1994, Cummaford and Stork in 2022, and Stork and Cummaford in 2022), and co-edited two books (with Baddeley in 1981 and Whitefield in 1989)[1].

The organisation and content of this book are something of a novel departure from these. They propose neither a framework (for the discipline of HCI as in Long and Dowell,

1989) nor a conception (for the design problem of HCI as in Dowell and Long, 1989)—both formative structures.

Rather, the current work offers a pre-formative structure by way of a guide to framing design practice for UX. The latter is based on an everyday language analysis of UX design practice concepts. These are expressed as descriptors, constituting an initial UX description. The latter is assessed against the UX practitioners' source materials to create a final such description and ways forward for UX.

About the Source Material and Its Contributors

The source material is contributed by successful UX practitioners. They are also versed in research as former colleagues and students of EU/UCL during my time as Director. The contributions appear from Chap. 4 onwards. Each complete contribution is posted on the website http://hciresearchforall.net. The source material contributors are listed below alphabetically by their surnames and are contactable directly.

Gerred Blyth

Degrees—B.A. (Hons) Psychology, University of Manchester; M.Sc., Human-Computer Interaction with Ergonomics, UCL.

Employment—Chief Product Officer, Giftory.com/*Contact* <gerred@gmail.com>

Seb Chakraborty

Degrees—B.Sc. Economics (Hons), Sussex; M.Sc., Knowledge Based Systems, Sussex; Applied Research, UCL.

Employment—Chief Product and Technology Officer Domestic and General/*Professional*—Chartered IT Professional (CTIP) and Fellow of British Computer Society (FBCS)/*Contact* <seb.chakraborty@gmail.com>

Steve Cummaford

Degrees—B.A. Philosophy, York; M.Sc. Cognitive Science, Cardiff; Ph.D., London (UCL).

Employment—Lead Digital Product Designer, Ted Baker; Lead UX Designer, Arcadia Group Ltd.; Lead UX Designer/Team Manager, SuperComfortable; Senior UX Designer, Vodafone Group; UX Design Specialist, JustGivin/*Contact* <cummaford@gmail.com>

Courtney Grant

Degrees—B.A. (Hons) Psychology; M.Sc. Human-Computer Interaction with Ergonomics, UCL.

Employment—Senior Engineer—Systems Performance and Integration (Human Factors), Transport for London/*Professional*—Chartered Fellow of the Chartered Institute of Ergonomics and Human Factors, European Ergonomist/*Contact* <clgonline@hotmail.com>

James Middlemass

Degrees—B.Sc. Business Administration and Human Psychology, Aston University, 1989; M.Sc. Ergonomics, UCL, 1992; Applied Research, UCL

Employment—BT; Business Analyst—Experience Design/*Contact* <james @ middlemass.com>

James Sinclair

Degrees—B.Sc. Economics, LSE; M.Sc. Philosophy, LSE; M.Sc. Human-Computer Interaction, UCL.

Employment—Tata, User Experience Consultant; Cheil, UX; HAVAS, Head UX; TMG Head of UCD/*Contact* <james@paperst.co.uk>

Peter Timmer

Degrees—B.Sc., Psychology, Warwick; M.Sc. Ergonomics, UCL; Ph.D., London (UCL).

Employment—Freelance Consultant and Managing Director, NOFORMULA LTD; Head of Experience, Fishawack; Head of UX, Blue Latitude Health; User Experience and Managing Director, Bisant Ltd.; Ux designer, Valtech/*Contact* <peter@bisant.com>

How This Book is Organised

First, the guide is expressed in terms of the everyday language used to describe design practice. This initial description of UX is composed of the resulting descriptors. For example, 'customers' and 'Internet website technology'. These can be expressed at lower levels of description. In this case, 'old/young' and 'specified/implemented'. Also, higher levels, 'humans' and 'digital technology'.

Second, the guide derives from the application of the initial UX description to UX practitioner source material to identify additional descriptors. Framing comprises any structures, used to support the conduct of UX design projects. These include frameworks, approaches, and methods. Also any structures to report design practice, such as case studies.

Third, identical descriptors from the initial description and the practitioner source materials are identified in the final UX description. Additional descriptors may also be included. Others may be excluded, depending on the potential users.

The book closes with two appendices of material for further learning. Appendix 1 is the carry forward of the initial description for framing UX design practice from Chaps. 1–3, and Appendix 2 is the same for Chap. 11.

Note that 'final description' is meant only as far as this guide is concerned. Further cycles of description development can be conducted. The guide constitutes an approach, but its associated method can be copied and developed. Alternative descriptions could be constructed, for example, for Consumer Experience (ConsX), Customer Experience (CustX), Experience-Centred Design Experience (ECD), Human Experience (HX), Human-Customer Experience (H-CustX), User-Customer Experience (UCustX) and UX.

This guide also delves into the background of UX as a movement, whose members seek to develop shared ideas for understanding and implementing user-computer technology as UX. Using the guide, practitioners and researchers can better relate current UX practice to their own. The ways forward for framing UX design practice in terms of this description can also be explored, identified, conceptualised and implemented, in particular with respect to Human-Computer Interaction (HCI), the starting point for much of current UX.

This book differs from other more top-down, formal and framework-driven books, proposing theories and prescriptions for UX. Those attempts to 'form' UX by fiat at this time appear to have had little effect. Further, the latter offers no specific address of the framing of UX design practice, its state and challenges. This book fills that gap.

In a dynamic field such as UX, there is seldom time to stop and think about the wider issues associated with the framing of design practice and related developments. This guide supports UX practitioners in identifying and reflecting on their design practice—what they are doing and why they are doing it. It also supports UX researchers to stop and to think about their research practice—what research they are conducting and how it is intended to support the framing of design practice for UX. Also, whether it is successful or not. The guide is also for undergraduate and graduate students seeking to understand the different ways of conducting and reporting UX. In addition, it provides grounding for young researchers trying to find their way in the fast developing, but preformed, world of UX.

The Rationale Behind This Book

A book such as this is much needed. It offers a way of relating UX design practice to UX research and both to HCI. The framings also contribute to the formation of UX in the longer term. Together, they offer a description, which UX practitioners can apply to reflect on their own practice. They can compare their work to that of their peers, for example, in terms of best-practice or business applications. Researchers can do likewise as concerns the knowledge they acquire, which is intended to support UX design practice. Also, the nature of that support and its success (or not) with respect to the needs of UX practitioners. The latter includes the range of different types of experience, for which design is desirable and possible.

The book differs from others about UX, its associated design knowledge, and the latter's application to practice. These tend to be theoretical, formative and prescriptive. In contrast, this book was written from the bottom-up perspective by reporting and analysing the design work of UX practitioners. The practice of those practitioners constitutes the source material of this book, and the relations between their practices are expressed as UX descriptors throughout the guide. Those relations can be understood, shared and taken forward by other practitioners and researchers by application of the same approach and development method.

The Intended Readership for This Book

The book is for people interested in, curious about, or generally trying to make sense of what is currently UX. For example, readers rather like myself and my former students, the latter of whom are now active in UX design practice. We asked ourselves whether UX is just HCI for Internet websites or simply an attempt to rebrand User-Centred Design (UCD). We even questioned if UX is replacing HCI and whether UX was the most important thing to be questioning at all. We came up with some answers. The book, however, does better.

More specifically, this guide is for graduate and postgraduate students of HCI and UX. It is also for young researchers (and their supervisors) seeking how best to support UX design practice. Given the diverse state of UX, and the lack of formation or consensus, UX presents a challenge. How can HCI researchers acquire and validate knowledge to support the framing of implicit UX design practice? Much of the current so-called HCI research into UX is little more than attempts at UX practice. The knowledge is implicit. It resides primarily in the design experience of the researcher/practitioner. However, it is not obvious how implicit knowledge can be built upon explicitly by other UX researchers. Development, then, is problematic.

The specific contribution of the book to HCI is to identify the relationship between UX and HCI, such as to support both HCI research and UX practice. The specific contribution of the book to the individual reader is to help them understand their work in terms of the HCI/UX descriptions. Also, to support that work and to suggest ways forward.

Exercise assignments in each chapter will help readers understand and practice framing UX design practice. This is especially useful to practitioners in related movements developing and sharing ideas contributing to UX and to HCI. These fields include cognitive psychology, design science, software engineering, lean design, design research, user-centred design, human-factors, cognitive engineering, human-computer interaction, agile design, cognitive ergonomics, experience-centred design and human-centred informatics.

London, UK   John Long

Acknowledgements

The book is a tribute to colleagues, M.Sc. and Ph.D. students of the EU/UCL Unit (University College London), both during my time as Director (1979–2001) and to the present. Starting as HCI researchers, their engagement with, and progress in, the world of UX design practice has made the book both desirable and possible. A group of them has contributed the practitioner source materials. Their motivation being fostered by long-term collaboration between one another and myself at EU/UCL. Of course, they will be able to cite their source materials in publications and on their CV. On a lighter note, at our annual EU/UCL reunion, they will also receive as many published copies of the book and pints of beer, to which the royalties will run.

Contents

Abbreviations

AI	Artificial Intelligence
CE	Customer Experience
CHI	Computer-Human Interaction
ConsX	Consumer Experience
CustX	Customer Experience
CX	Consumer Experience
ECD	Experience-Centred Design Experience
HCE	Human-Customer Experience
HCI	Human-Computer Interaction
H-CustX	Human-Customer Experience
HE	Human Experience
HX	Human Experience
UC	Customer Experience
UE	User Experience
UX	User Experience

Initial Description for UX

1

1.1 User

User is characterised in terms of general and UX user.

1.1.1 General

A 'user' is someone, who 'uses something to do something, as intended'. For example, a carpenter uses a saw, to cut wood to size. Wikipedia distinguishes physical tools, such as a hammer, from abstract tool-like processes, such as a mathematical French curve. There are many kinds of tool—domestic appliances, educational devices, human–computer technology and logics.

1.1.2 UX User

The notion of use and of tool are combined.

Carry-forward to the initial UX description is 'a user is someone, who uses human–computer technology to do something as intended.' For example, friends use smartphones to enjoy exchanging news.

1.2 Experience

Experience is characterised in terms of general and UX experience.

© The Author(s), under exclusive license to Springer Nature Switzerland AG 2025
J. Long, *Guide to Framing Design Practice for UX*, Synthesis Lectures
on Human-Centered Informatics, https://doi.org/10.1007/978-3-031-68981-9_1

1.2.1 General

'Experience' means a conscious event, as in perception and emotion. For example, seeing and enjoying a sunrise. It also means the knowledge and skills resulting from such events, for example, as in the coaching and playing of sport. UX designers' experience includes the skills of sketching images and structuring text. Wikipedia distinguishes six kinds of experience—physical, mental, emotional, spiritual, social and virtual. Additional types of experiences include aesthetics (as in beauty), conflict (as in destructive relations), friendship (as in ties to others), mortality (as in death) and self-fulfilment (as in pride of self).

1.2.2 UX Experience

The notion of conscious events and that of the knowledge and skills derived from them are combined.

Carry-forward is 'conscious events and the knowledge and skills derived from them.' For example, friendship may increase as the result of smartphone fun communications.

1.3 User Experience

User experience is characterised in terms of general and UX user experience.

1.3.1 General

'User experience' has evolved from the original HCI (Human–Computer Interaction) idea of usability, as experience. It now includes 'well-being' and many others. In UX, it is inclusive, vying with HCI itself. For example, in Internet applications and with website designers. Definitions tend to be general—strong on inclusivity, but weaker for operationalisation, as required to frame UX design practice. The latter needs to be complete enough to be inclusive, but exclusive enough to be operationalised [1].

1.3.2 UX User Experience

User and experience are combined.

Carry-forward is 'conscious events and the knowledge and skills derived from them, which result in a user experience for someone, who uses human–computer technology to do something, as intended'. For example, activist groups use smartphones the better to organise their campaigns [2].

1.4   Movement

Movement is characterised in terms of general and UX movement.

1.4.1   General

User experience characterises a type of professional change, which can take the form of a 'movement'. The latter denotes a group of people working together to advance shared ideas concerning user experience.

1.4.2   UX Movement

UX is a group of people working together to advance shared UX ideas. UX practitioners design human–computer technology for user experience. The technology includes smartphones. The latter may constitute a pleasurable experience (and memory) for such users, as well as better communication skills (see 1.2.2).

Carry-forward is 'professional change and development of UX practitioners working together to advance shared ideas'. Practitioners may claim allegiance to customer or human customer 'wings' of such a movement.

1.5   Problem

Problem is characterised in terms of general and UX problem.

1.5.1   General

The shared ideas, which a UX movement seeks to advance, are too high-level to be useful. They must relate to practitioners' design of human–computer technology and its impact on people and their organisations.

1.5.2   UX Problem

Experience 'requirements' is one expression for the UX problem. They might include experiences such as well-being and frustration to be satisfied by the technology. However, if the former is considered a solution, then some notion of problem is a necessary antecedent. Taken together, problem and solution can both be related to the design of human–computer technology. Also to the understanding of the place and impact of interactive technology, for example, in hospitals, service industries and schools, much in the way espoused by experience-centred design (ECD—McCarthy & Wright, 2004). Both the design and understanding of experience are precursors of the initial description of UX. In any doubt, both should be assumed. The definition of UX problem and solution, then, is a way of describing the shared ideas, which practitioners are working together to advance, in a movement (1.4.1).

Carry-forward is 'user experience problem and user experience solution, which describe the shared user experience ideas, which practitioners are working together to advance'.

1.6   General Problem

General problem is characterised in terms of general and UX general problem.

1.6.1   General

A general problem is one, which contains more than one type of problem, each associated with one or more solutions.

Carry-forward is 'UX general problems associated with UX general solutions, which describe the shared ideas, which practitioners are working together to advance'.

1.6.2   UX General Problem

A UX general problem is one, which contains more than one type of UX problem each associated with one or more UX solutions.

Carry-forward is 'UX general problems each associated with UX general solutions, which describe the shared ideas, which practitioners are working together to advance'.

1.7   General Design Problem

General design problem is characterised in terms of general and UX general design problem.

1.7.1   General

A 'general design problem' is one, which contains more than one type of design problem, each associated with one or more design solutions (1.6.1).

1.7.2   UX General Design Problem

The UX general design problems and general design solutions together constitute the 'UX general design problem'.

Carry-forward is 'UX general design problem is to specify and to implement human–computer technology for a user as someone, who uses human–computer technology to do something, as intended, which results in experience comprising conscious events and the knowledge and skills derived from them.'

1.8   Particular Scope

Particular scope is characterised in terms of general and UX particular scope.

1.8.1   General

Problem and solution describe generally the shared ideas, which practitioners are working together to advance. The expression is sufficiently inclusive of user experience, such as fun and exclusive such as genetic makeup (at least to date).

1.8.2   UX Particular Scope

Problem and solution typically address matters in hand or concerns. They can be said to have a 'scope', that is, a range over which they apply.

Carry-forward is 'UX particular scope of UX design problem and UX design solution to specify and to implement human–computer technology for users as people, who use human–computer technology to do something as intended, which results in an experience comprising conscious events and the knowledge and skills derived from them'.

1.9   State of UX General Design Problem and UX Particular Scope

Carry-forward is 'UX general design problem and UX particular scope to specify and to implement human–computer technology for user experience' (1.8.2).

1.10   Critique and Challenge for UX General Design Problem and U$x Particular Scope

Carry-forward is 'UX general design problem and UX particular scope to specify and to implement human–computer technology for user experience' (1.8.2).

1.11   UX Research

'UX research' acquires and validates UX knowledge to support UX practice, as research more generally (1.7). Unlike disciplines, such as science and engineering, however, UX currently constitutes a movement. Hence, UX research needs to acquire and to validate implicit as well as explicit design knowledge. The latter comprises the UX ideas that practitioners are working together to advance. Their expression is in terms of problem and particular scope. Knowledge, acquired by UX research, includes the conduct and reporting of different types of design practice and their supporting structures. The reporting includes types of communication. Such research has much in common with that employing qualitative methods and attempting to understand the impact of technology on people and their organisations, such as schools and care homes as in ECD (Experience Centred Design) (McCarthy & Wright, 2004). Also including research attempting to generalise from context-rich case studies (Polit & Beck, 2010).

   Carry-forward is 'acquisition and validation of implicit UX knowledge and explicit UX knowledge to support UX design practice.'

Chapter Review

The chapter proposes a basis for the initial UX description. The latter is expressed in terms of everyday language. It comprises—user, experience, user experience, movement, problem, general problem, general design problem, particular scope, state, critique and challenge and research.

Chapter Carry Forward

The carry-forward from this chapter and Chaps. 2 and 3 appears in Appendix 1. It constitutes the basis for the initial UX description and so for the guide to framing design practice for UX. The appendix is intended to support readers in applying the initial UX description to the practitioner source material, presented in Chaps. 4–10. Also, in completing the associated exercise assignments. Appendix 1 is not for reading as a text in itself, but for consultation in its application.

1.12   Exercise Assignment

The exercise assignment is intended to test readers' understanding and application of the concepts presented. Also to support tailoring the initial UX description to their own design requirements.

Consulting 1.1 User

- *Add* any points to the text content, which you think should have been included. These can include additional concepts, definitions, descriptors and clarifications. Cite the work you are using. Justify any such additions with your reasons.
- *Edit* the carry forward proposals in the light of any additions to the text content, which you consider to be appropriate.
- *Justify* any such edits with your reasons.

Editing can easily be done on digital copies but also with different coloured highlight markers on hard copies.

Consult and

- *Complete* the following sections as for 1.1

1.2 Experience; 1.3 User Experience; 1.4 Movement; 1.5 Problem; 1.6 General Problem; 1.7 General Design Problem; 1.8 Particular Scope; 1.9 State of UX General Design Problem and UX Particular Scope; 1.10 Critique and Challenge for UX General Design Problem and UX Particular Scope; 1.11 UX Research.

Consult Note [1] below and appended to 1.1.3.

- *Can* the threads of McCarthy and Wright be synthesised with the carry forward of 1.1.3 as a lower level of description? If so, attempt to create specific and detailed illustrations.

- *Note* any difficulties, which you experience.
- *Why* might this be so?
- *Give* your reasons, if you do not think synthesis is possible.
- *What* changes to either might facilitate synthesis?

1.13   Notes

[1] The balance between being complete enough to be inclusive, but exclusive enough to be operationalised, is hard to achieve. Raising the level of description favours completeness and so exclusivity. At the same time, it makes operationalisation more difficult. Lowering the level of description has the reverse effect.

[2] Readers might like to consider the proposed carry forward with the four threads of experience presented by McCarthy and Wright (2004) in their attempt to understand the impact interactive technology has on the experiences of people and their social organisations. The threads are sensual ('is concerned with our sensory engagement with a situation, which orients us to the concrete, palpable, and visceral character of experience'); emotional ('refers to value judgements, that ascribe to other people and things importance with respect to our needs and desires'); compositional ('is concerned with relationships between the parts and the whole of an experience') and spatio-temporal ('space and time pervade our language of experience... experiences of space and time are constructed through interaction... space and time may be connected or disconnected...'). See also the associated exercise assignment (1.8).

References

McCarthy, J., & Wright, P. (2004). *Technology as experience.* MIT Press.
Polit, D., & Beck, C. (2010). Generalization in quantitative and qualitative research: Myths and strategies. *International Journal of Nursing Studies, 47*(11), 1451–1458.

Initial Description for UX Design Practice 2

2.1 Design

Design is characterised in terms of general and UX design.

2.1.1 General

A design in everyday language is a plan or drawing. It shows the look and function of an artefact, before it is made. Such artefacts include buildings, clothes and other objects. Synonyms include sketch, outline and model. For example, architects produce plans of buildings, which are built. Fashion designers produce an artist's impression of dresses, which are made up and sewn.

Carry-forward is 'design representation' [1].

2.1.2 UX Design

UX design is typically expressed as a user journey, page layout and so on. It shows the look and function of an application before its implementation. Such applications include planning and control systems and health guides. Synonyms include interface sketch and initial version. For example, UX practitioners produce alternative versions of educational interfaces for different types of students. Software engineers produce animations for synthesis with different applications.

Carry-forward is 'UX design representation' [1].

© The Author(s), under exclusive license to Springer Nature Switzerland AG 2025   9
J. Long, *Guide to Framing Design Practice for UX*, Synthesis Lectures
on Human-Centered Informatics, https://doi.org/10.1007/978-3-031-68981-9_2

2.2   Practice

Practice is characterised in terms of general and UX practice.

2.2.1   General

Practice has two meanings. First, a job or business, involving skill or training and by implication performance. For example, a medical practice at which a doctor treats patients. Second, the act of doing something regularly to improve one's skill and performance. For example, sports practice, as in football or tennis.

*Carry-forw*ard is 'practice and performance'. The definition denotes both skill and training, also the act of doing something repeatedly to improve one's skill.

2.2.2   UX Practice

UX practice also has two meanings. First, a job or business, such as that of a consultant or agent. Both involve skill, training and performance. For example, a practice in which a designer creates applications. Second, the act of doing something regularly to improve one's skill. For example, online game-playing practice, as in chess and shoot-to-kill applications.

Carry-forward is 'UX practice and UX performance, as both skill and training. Also the act of doing something regularly or repeatedly to improve one's skill in so doing.'

2.3   Design Practice

Design practice is characterised in terms of general and UX design practice.

2.3.1   General

'Design practice' is a term used in engineering. For example, as in mechanical and electronic engineering. The former involves specifying and implementing artefacts such as locomotive piston rods. The latter involves artefacts such as electrical undersea cables.

Design practice in everyday language conjoins aspects of two concepts—'representation and performance in response to a brief'. Representation can be expressed as 'specify representation'. Performance can be expressed as 'implement representation' [2].

Carry-forward is 'specify representations and design performance as implement representations'.

2.3.2 UX Design Practice

Carry-forward is 'specify UX representations and UX performance as implement UX representations' (2.3.1).

2.4 State of UX Design Practice

Much of UX design knowledge is implicit, residing in the experience of the practitioner. Explicit UX design knowledge in the form of standards, guidelines and published best-practice is at best 'work-in-progress'. Some UX practitioners are content for this to remain so. They believe design cannot be so prescribed. Others would adopt some explicit design knowledge, were it to be effective.

Carry-forward is 'specify UX representations and UX design performance as implement UX representations'.

2.5 Critique and Challenge for UX Design Practice

The critique and challenge for UX design practice is the same as for the state of UX design practice (2.4).

Carry-forward is 'specify UX representations and UX design performance as implement UX representations'.

2.6 UX Design Practice Research

'UX design practice research' acquires and validates UX knowledge to support UX practice, just like research more generally (1.7). UX research comprises the ideas that UX practitioners are working together to advance. UX design practice knowledge, acquired by UX research, includes the conduct and reporting of UX design practice. The former includes 'specify UX representations and implement UX representations'. The latter includes different types of UX practice, including their support structures and types of communication.

Carry-forward is 'acquisition and validation of implicit UX knowledge and explicit UX knowledge to support UX design practice' [3].

Chapter Review

The chapter proposes a basis for the initial UX description. The latter is expressed in everyday language. It comprises—design, UX design, practice, UX practice, design practice, UX design practice state, critique and challenge and UX design practice research.

Chapter Carry Forward

The carry-forward from Chaps. 1–3 appears in Appendix 1. It constitutes the basis for the initial UX description and so for the guide to framing design practice for UX. The appendix is intended to support readers in applying the initial UX description to the practitioner source material, presented in Chaps. 4–10. Also, in completing the associated exercise assignments. Appendix 1 is not for reading as a text in itself, but for consultation for its application.

2.7   Exercise Assignment

The exercise assignment is intended to test readers' understanding and application of the concepts presented. Also to support tailoring the initial UX description to their own design requirements.

Consulting 2.1 Design

– *Add* any points to the text content, which you think should have been included. These can include additional concepts, definitions, descriptors and clarifications. Cite the work you are using to complete the assignment. Justify any such additions with your reasons.
– *Edit* the carry-forward proposals in the light of any additions to the text content.
– *Justify* any such edits with your reasons.

Editing can be done on digital copies. Also with different coloured highlight markers on hard copies.

Consult and

– *Complete* the following sections as for 2.1.

2.2 Practice; 2.3 Design Practice; 2.4 State of UX Design Practice; 2.5 Critique and Challenge for UX Design Practice; 2.6 UX Design Practice Research.

2.8   Notes

[1] 'Design' here describes the product of designing. Consistently, the latter would be the creation of design representations.
[2] 'Implement' has two senses. The first is manufacture for commercial distribution. The second is less 'final'. It might refer to a design as an initial version in the form of a prototype. Unless indicated otherwise, the second meaning is assumed here.

Initial Description for Framing UX Design Practice

3

3.1 Framing

Framing is characterised in terms of general and framing UX.

3.1.1 General

The general description of framing is the application of structures. The latter include framework, approach, method and case study. The structures frame issues and problems for the purposes of thinking and doing something about them. Also, reporting what has been done and how well.

The structures support expression of the question or issue, for example, in the form of a project. Framework is the more formal and approach less so. Method indicates how a project is carried out. A case study reports the outcomes of a project. All are structures.

Carry-forward is 'framing as application of structures'.

3.1.2 Framing UX

Framing UX structures includes—UX framework, UX approach, UX method and UX case study. They are addressed next.

3.1.2.1 As Concerns Framework

As concerns framework, framing denotes a structure—the frame. For example, painters use wooden frames to hang their portraits. UX designers use colours to frame banner adverts. A physical border supports and so delimits something, as in the case of a picture

© The Author(s), under exclusive license to Springer Nature Switzerland AG 2025   13
J. Long, *Guide to Framing Design Practice for UX*, Synthesis Lectures
on Human-Centered Informatics, https://doi.org/10.1007/978-3-031-68981-9_3

or window. A window frame can be made of metal. UX designers use lines to emphasise product special offers. Also, that of a structure to which parts are added, as in the case of a building or vehicle. For example, wheels and pedals are added to the frame of a bicycle. Likewise, UX designers add links to sitemaps 'Long et al. (2022a, b)'.

In addition, frame has an abstract meaning of organisation, as the way objects are put together or constructed. For example, a statistical model made of lines and boxes. UX practitioners construct a sitemap to optimise uplift.

Framework implicates framing.

Carry-forward is 'framework as application of structures for frame and framing'.

3.1.2.2 As Concerns Approach

As concerns approach, framing denotes an action or manner of taking steps to attain a goal. The latter may be designing or constructing something physical or abstract.

The first physical meaning is that of scope, which delimits something, as in the case of design or construction. For example, a UX keyboard prototype to enter digitised data. The second is that of a structure to which parts may be added, as in the case of a UX communications network.

In addition, approach has the abstract meaning of perspective, as the way of viewing something. For example, an analytical, as opposed to, an empirical perspective. The former may be organising a set of images to promote the sales of domestic appliances. Approach implicates scope, structure and perspective.

Carry-forward is 'approach as application of structures having scope, structure and perspective'.

3.1.2.3 As Concerns Method

As concerns method, it denotes a procedure or a technique for attaining a goal. These means are supported by methodological or 'how' knowledge. The contrast is with declarative, substantive or 'what' knowledge. The degree of a method's support depends on its effectiveness. That is the confidence it affords the successful attainment of its goal. UX designers apply best-practice methods.

Carry-forward is 'method as application of types of method structure'.

Three main types of method have been identified (Dowell & Long, 1989). They are 'implement and test', 'specify and implement' and 'specify then implement'.

'Implement and Test' began life as 'trial and error' in the psychology learning literature. Rats in laboratory experiments succeed in learning the way through a maze, but only after trying other incorrect ways. Their initial knowledge of the maze is insufficient to support a quicker process. 'Implement and Test' is a comparable UX method.

Carry-forward is 'application of structures as implement and test'.

'Specify and implement' characterises UX design practice, if the specification can be implicit. It assumes design knowledge sufficient to support the initial specification of the artefact to be implemented.

Carry-forward is 'application of structures as specify and implement'.

'Specify then implement' requires design knowledge not only to support the initial specification of the artefact, but also its implementation, without further test of the knowledge itself. Not a UX method at this time. It is included for completeness.

Carry-forward is 'application of structures as specify then implement'.

3.1.2.4 As Concerns Case Study

As concerns case study, it denotes an in-depth observation of an instance of a complex issue in its real-life context. Instances may include one person, a group or an event. The UX case study analyses instances to seek patterns and relationships between them. Generalising such instances, however, is not straightforward (Polit & Beck, 2010).

Carry-forward is 'application of structures as in organising and reporting a case study'.

3.2 Framing Design

'Design' is first characterised in general, then described with respect to UX. Similarly, for the UX structures of framework, approach, method and case study.

3.2.1 General

Carry-forward is 'design representation' (2.1.1). This mediates the act or manner of applying structures of framework, approach, method and case study to framing a user of human–computer technology to do something, as intended. The latter results in an experience comprising conscious events and the knowledge and skills derived from them (1.1.1–2).

3.2.2 Framing UX Design

A UX designer uses an existing framework, approach and method to put together a UX method. The latter is specific to a domain of application new to the practitioner. The UX structures are to be used in a project. The latter involves the redesign of an e-commerce website offering an Internet banking service. The UX designer wants to increase the trust experience of the customer. The UX method, supported by the UX framework and the UX approach, is 'implement and test'.

Carry-forward is 'UX design representation'. This mediates the process or manner of application of structures of UX framework, UX approach, UX method and UX case study. The latter for framing a user of human–computer technology to do something, as intended. This results in an experience comprising conscious events and the knowledge and skills derived from them (1.1.1–2).

3.3   Framing Practice

'Framing practice' is first described in general. Then with respect to UX.

3.3.1   General

Carry-forward is 'practice as performance'. This mediates the process or manner of applying structures as framework, approach, method and case study for framing a user of human–computer technology to do something, as intended. The latter results in an experience comprising conscious events and the knowledge and skills derived from them.

3.3.2   Framing UX Practice

A UX designer uses an existing UX framework, UX approach and UX method (to be the object of a case study report) to put together a UX method for a domain new to the practitioner. The UX structures are to be used in a project involving the redesign of an e-commerce website, selling beauty products. The new design is to increase the aesthetic experience of the purchaser. The UX method, supported by the UX framework and UX approach is that of 'implement and test'.

    Carry-forward is 'application of structures of UX framework, UX approach, UX method and UX case study'. This mediates framing a user of human–computer technology to do something, as intended. The latter results in an experience comprising conscious events and the knowledge and skills derived from them.

3.4   Framing Design Practice

'Design practice' is first characterised in general, then described with respect to UX.

3.4.1   General

Carry-forward is 'specify representations and implement representations' (2.3.1). This mediates the act or process of providing a framework, an approach or a method for framing a user of human–computer technology to do something, as intended. The latter results in an experience comprising conscious events and the knowledge and skills derived from them (1.1.1–2).

3.4.2 Framing UX Design Practice

A UX designer uses an existing UX framework, a UX approach and a UX method (to be the object of a case study report) to put together a UX method for a domain new to the practitioner. The latter for a project involving the redesign of an e-commerce website, selling 'safe' children's toys. The new design is to increase the pleasure experience of the child and the safety confidence of the parent. The UX method, supported by the UX framework and UX approach, is to be 'specify then implement'. However, the UX practitioner is unable to find such a method. Instead, 'implement and test' is applied and reported.

Carry-forward is 'specify UX representations and implement UX representations by application of UX structures of UX framework, UX approach, UX method and UX case study'. This mediates framing a user of human–computer technology to do something, as intended. The latter results in an experience comprising conscious events and the knowledge and skills derived from them.

3.5 State of Framing UX Design Practice

Most UX framing, both in its conduct and reporting, is implicit in the experience of UX practitioners. The latter may also be influenced by their employer organisation and best-practice. Explicit UX design practice framing in the form of standards, guidelines and published best-practice has yet to be created (and so validated). Some UX practitioners are content for this to continue, as design cannot be so prescribed. Others are not against framing design practice support were the latter to be effective. The current state of framing UX design practice, then, is determined by the practitioner doing the framing in terms of their UX design knowledge and experience.

Carry-forward is 'specify UX representations and UX design performance as implement UX representations'.

3.6 Critique and Challenge for Framing UX Design Practice

The critique and challenge of UX framing of design practice is essentially the same as for the state of framing UX design practice (3.5).

Carry-forward is 'specify UX representations and UX design performance as implement UX representations'.

3.7   Framing UX Design Practice Research

Framing UX design practice research acquires and validates knowledge to support practice research, as such research generally (1.7 and 2.6). Hence, the latter acquires and validates implicit as well as explicit such knowledge. This includes the ideas that UX practitioners are working together to advance. This includes the reporting thereof. The former includes the structures of framework, approach and method. The latter includes the following types of method—'implement and test', 'specify and implement' and 'specify then implement' (to be complete). The UX reporting may take the form of a case study.

Carry-forward is 'UX conduct and UX reporting'. UX conduct comprises the structures of framework, approach and method. The latter include 'implement and test', 'specify and implement' and 'specify then implement'. UX reporting comprises case studies.

Chapter Review

The chapter proposes a basis for the initial UX description. The latter is expressed in terms of everyday language. It comprises—framing, framework, approach, method, case study, framing UX, UX framework, UX approach, UX method, UX case study, framing design, framing UX design, framing practice, framing UX practice, framing design practice, framing UX design practice, state, critique and challenge and UX design practice research.

Chapter Carry Forward

The carry-forward from Chaps. 1–3 appears in Appendix 1. It constitutes the basis for the initial UX description and hence for the guide to framing design practice for UX. The appendix is intended to support readers in applying the initial UX description to the UX practitioner source material, presented in Chaps. 4–10. Also, in completing the associated exercise assignments. Appendix 1 is not for reading as a text in itself, but for consultation in its application.

3.8   Exercise Assignment

The exercise assignment is intended to test readers' understanding and application of the concepts presented. Also to support tailoring the initial UX description to their own design requirements.

Consulting 3.1 General

– *Add* any points to the text content, which you think should have been included. Cite the work you are using to complete the assignment. Justify any such additions with your reasons.
– *Edit* the carry-forward proposals in the light of any additions to the text content. Justify any such edits with your reasons.

Consult and

Complete the following sections as for 3.1

3.2 Framing Design; 3.3 Framing Practice; 3.4 Framing Design Practice; 3.5 State of Framing UX Design Practice; 3.6 Critique and Challenge for Framing UX Design Practice and Framing UX Design Practice Research.

3.9 Notes

[1] 'Specify, then implement' as a method is included here for completeness.
[2] How to operationalise 'specify, then implement' method design knowledge would of necessity need to be explicit. This would be the case whether intended for application by UX or HCI practitioners.

References

Dowell, J., & Long, J. (1989). Target paper: Conception of the cognitive engineering design problem. *Ergonomics, 41*(2), 126–139.
Long, J., Cummaford, S., & Stork, A. (2022a). *HCI design knowledge—Critique, challenge and a way forward.* Springer Nature.
Long, J., Stork, A., & Cummaford, S. (2022b). *Towards engineering design principles for HCI.* Springer Nature.
Polit, D., & Beck, C. (2010). Generalization in quantitative and qualitative research: Myths and strategies. *International Journal of Nursing Studies, 47*(11), 1451–1458.

UX Practitioner Source Material Describing UX in General

4

4.1   Introduction

The guide combines the initial UX descriptors with the descriptors from the UX practitioner contributions to produce the final UX description. The combination is achieved by means of the UX guide notes. The original UX contributions vary in length. They may be divided in the guide, according to their content. Each chapter and source material contribution has its own summary and review. To crosscheck the UX contributions with the initial UX descriptors, see Appendix 1.

UX guide notes link the source materials to the initial UX description. The links have different functions. Those between the source material and the guide notes identify the specific relation between the two in terms of descriptors. These can be expressed at different levels. The links also identify the same descriptors appearing in the initial UX description and the associated source material. They are shown in **Bold**, with the initial letter capitalised, for example, **User** and **User Experience**. They appear only in the UX source material and only once to avoid individual source material contributor bias. The exception is 'UX', which is not shown in bold. This is because its constant use throughout would only be a distraction. Further, the links identify the different, and so additional, descriptors appearing in the source material. They are shown in *Italics* with the initial letter capitalised, for example, *Website* and *Human–Computer Technology*. Last, links relate the guide comments to the initial UX descriptors. The first letter of each word is capitalised as in 'Design' and 'Human–Computer Interaction'.

The source material descriptors and the initial UX description may be related directly or indirectly. Direct relations hold between the same descriptors, for example, UX and Ux. These both denote 'user experience'. Alternatively, the descriptors may be the same (or very similar), but use different terms, for example, 'website screen' and 'website page'. Further, the descriptors may be relational, for example, 'HCI as UX'. The relationship

© The Author(s), under exclusive license to Springer Nature Switzerland AG 2025   21
J. Long, *Guide to Framing Design Practice for UX*, Synthesis Lectures
on Human-Centered Informatics, https://doi.org/10.1007/978-3-031-68981-9_4

may be hierarchical by abstraction or categorical by generification. Such relations may be the object of the guide notes by association with the initial UX description.

The source material is sufficient to construct a final UX description with respect to the initial everyday language description. The two are relative to one another and of like kind. Hence, the reader is warned about the difficulties of generalisation (Polit & Beck, 2010).

4.2   Welcome to the World of UX

4.2.1   Sinclair Source Material (2023)

'I love design, data, making things and then making them better. I'm lucky that I do UX. I love the simplicity of the idea at its core—Test and Iterate.

I've been doing this for the past 20 years for more organisations than you can shake a stick at. Everywhere I have been, as a Head of UX, I have set up a lab. This is the easiest and most effective way to get a design mind-set into an organisation and build client trust in a solution. And the most creative part of the *Design Process* happens when you put users in front of a product. The friction between the product and the user is where novel solutions emerge.

I nurture talent and build teams of skilled and dedicated UXers that have fun and produce great work. I provide them with space and time to think by Uxing UX, creating tools and processes to raise standards and save time.'

4.2.2   Chakraborty Source Material (2023)

'The topic of UX is complex and struggles with definition, scope, and perceived utility. At the same time, everyone wants it, feels it's important and yet no-one completely owns it. Experience is unique; mine is mine and yours is yours and yet design would get quite complicated without some commonality, a set of norms, rules of thumb or good old-fashioned principles'.

Guide Note

Sinclair and Chakraborty's source material for UX in general are presented in full later. The extracts are just to set the scene for this chapter. Sinclair's is a pure 'hurray' for UX. Chakraborty's is more circumspect. Together they express the current differences within UX, the object of the guide's address.

4.3   Grant Source Material (2023)

Summary

Grant's source material is 'pre-UX'. He understands HCI as UCD. He does not use the term UX. The contribution, however, belongs in the guide. It adds to usability the experiences of well-being, pleasure, frustration and discomfort. It recognises the importance of experience for framing design practice as in the manner of UCD. The similarities and differences with UX contributions are instructive. Grant's source material comprises sections on—Education, Employment, Project Work and Safety Critical Environments.

4.3.1   Education

According to Grant, 'He completed his MSc in *Human–Computer Interaction with Ergonomics*. The course provided the foundation for a career in *User-Centred Design* (*UCD*).'

Guide Notes

Human–Computer Interaction with Ergonomics, as a descriptor, denotes the field of study/ discipline, associated with the world of work.

User-Centred Design (*UCD*) links to the carry-forward of UX as a Movement (1.4.2). If User Experience (1.3.2) is considered part of *UCD*, and so not a uniquely UX descriptor, then UX is a Movement (1.4.2). If parity between *UCD* and UX is presumed, then both are Movements (1.4.2). Alternatively, they are just ways of doing HCI. If parity does not hold, then one is superordinate to the other.

4.3.2   Employment

'Following engineering consultancy, as a *Human Factors* **Practitioner** (1.5.2), work included both physical and software *Ergonomics* in multi-disciplinary design teams in defence, nuclear, and rail. Further work included safety assurance projects. The rigorous approach of such projects was formative and influenced the subsequent framing of *Human Factors* design **Practice** (2.2.1).'

Guide Notes

Human Factors, as a descriptor, is an alternative to *Ergonomics*, both in the US and UK.

Practitioner (1.5.2) refers to someone practising *Human Factors* design.

Ergonomics implies that software *Ergonomics*, as *UCD*, is an alternative to UX as a way of conducting *Human–Computer Interaction*.

4.3.3   Project Work

'*Pleasurable* experience is considered critical to both systems **Performance** (2.2.1) and personnel *Wellbeing*. For example, Users (1.1.2) on a major control room project reported how much better they found the communication flows in the upgraded control room. The changes improved the way Users (1.1.2) worked. The changes also made the *Environment* more *Pleasurable* in which to work.'

Guide Notes

Pleasure, as a descriptor, denotes a positive Experience (1.3.2), as related to systems Performance (2.2.1). Here, it derives from *Human Factors/UCD* rather than from UX.

   Experience (1.3.2) is exemplified only as *Pleasure* and *Wellbeing*. They are addressed at a high level. The claimed UX range of possible experiences is much greater.

   Wellbeing is a positive experiential state of mind and body. The contrast is with not *Wellbeing*. Both can be engendered by conditions at *Work*—physical, mental and social.

   Users (1.1.2) apply Human–Computer Technology (1.3.2) to do something as desired and intentional.

   Pleasure/Wellbeing—see earlier.

4.3.4   Safety Critical Environments

'It is critical to collect feedback from *End*-Users (1.1.2) to understand their views about the systems they use. In safety-critical environments, *Users* (1.1.2) have to persevere with such systems over the long-term. They cannot simply change to alternative systems. If the former are not designed for their needs, *Frustration* and *Discomfort* result. Understanding the **User Experience** (1.2.2) is supported by maintaining an issues log. This captures **User** (1.1.2) feedbac*k*, which is then mapped to specific parameters. The latter can then be used to help determine, whether the actions taken to resolve the issue successfully, improve the User Experience (1.2.2).'

Guide Notes

Users (1.1.2), as a descriptor, are people, who use Human–Computer Technology (1.3.2) to do something as desired and intended.

   Frustration increases User Experiences (1.2.2), as identified by the source material. *Frustration* is typically the result of not performing work as desired. *Frustration* may be experienced by the worker, the supervisor or associated *Stakeholders*.

   Discomfort likewise increases User Experiences (1.2.2). The number of experiences mentioned, however, remains modest compared to the UX potential.

Identical Descriptors

Practitioner (1.5.2/User (1.1.2)/User Experience (1.2.2)/Performance (2.2.1)/Practice

Additional Descriptors

HCI with Ergonomics/UCD/Work/Environment/Human Factors/Practitioners/Pleasure/

Frustration/Discomfort/Stakeholders

Review

Grant's position, concerning UX in general, is to claim 'user experience' as part of UCD/ HCI and so continuity between UCD/HCI and UX. This is typical of HCI practitioners, who are not ready to 'jump the UCD/HCI ship' for UX. He also welcomes comparable UCD/HCI formation for 'user experience'. This mixed HCI/UX relationship is the source of much disagreement and associated lack of consensus between the two. They illustrate the motivation for the guide. Many UX identical descriptors are shared—five in all. More than many straight UX contributions. Many more, however, are relational, primarily of the subordinate kind. The absence of UCD from the UX description may be the reason. Hence, the absence of reference to the higher levels of description, as might relate to user experience general problem and user experience specific scope. The deficit might be made good as relational to human–computer technology, as associated with HCI. Like-wise, research as related to user experience research, user experience knowledge and user experience design practice.

4.4   Chakraborty Source Material (2023)

Summary

Chakraborty's source material is 'current UX', that is ongoing. It comprises sections on— Topic and associated Key Ideas. Also, its current struggles, as concern definition, scope and perceived utility. UX in general is considered not to be well-specified. Better UX formation, then, is welcomed to help make good the absence of consensus.

4.4.1   UX as a Topic

'The *Topic* of UX is complex and struggles with *Definition, Scope* and *Perceived Utility*. At the same time, everyone wants it, feels it's important and yet no-one completely owns it. **Experience** (1.2.2) is unique; mine is mine and yours is yours…'

Guide Notes

Topic of UX, as a descriptor, could be a UX superordinate. Perhaps more like the 'whole idea of' or the 'subject matter of'. Additionally, *Topic* might identify a field of study [3].

However, it is not an alternative to Movement (1.4.2), which implicates UX Practitioners (1.5.2). (Topic also relates to the User Experience General Problem (1.7.2). It denotes the range over which UX operates.

UX denotes User Experience (1.2.2).

Definition is required to specify UX. The 'struggle' derives from different views on its structure and content. Also, to the vagueness and absence of such views. Source material provides ample evidence on the lack of consensus as to what constitutes UX (what it is—its ontology and what it does—its epistemology). Also, the lack of consensus concerning its Practice (2.2.1).

Perceived Utility implies different ways of viewing UX. It might relate to user intention. It is certainly a criterion of interactive system Performance (2.3.1). A more formed expression of UX would require the scoping of its concepts, such as *Topic, Definition* and *Perceived Utility*.

(User) Experience (1.2.2) is the primary and foundational descriptor of UX. Individual Conscious Events (1.2.2) are, of course, unique. However, they can still be designed for (whether successfully or not) and their effects on social organisations understood in the manner of ECD. Also, to be one of the shared ideas the UX Movement (1.4.2) is working to advance. Users (1.1.2) may have the same intent, at some level of description, for example paying a bill by Internet banking. But the individual Experience (1.2.2) of realising that specific intent is unique and individual.

4.4.2   UX Key Ideas

(1) 'UX is dead, long live UX.
(2) How does a *Product-Centric Frame* for UX help?
(3) How do you do UX at speed in the *Era of Exponential*?'

Guide Notes

UX, as a descriptor, is strikingly juxtaposed as being both dead and alive. Most practitioners would claim one or the other. The description underlines disagreements within the UX Movement (1.4.2). Also, the difficulties of specifying its *Definition, Scope* and *Perceived Utility*. Chakraborty welcomes a better formation of UX.

Product-Centric Frame is novel and links to business, markets, management and to *Perceived Utility*. It contrasts with user-centric and consumer-centric framing and Design practice (1.11).

Era of Exponential refers to the rate at which new digital technology is developed, the speed of its market penetration and the range of its applications. *At Speed* in conjunction with *Era of Exponential*, poses a greater challenge for UX.

Identical Descriptors

Experience (1.2.2).

Additional Descriptors

UX/Topic of UX/Definition/Perceived Utility/Product-Centric Frame/Era of Exponential.

Review

Chakraborty's position concerning UX in general is that better UX formation is to be welcomed. He considers UX to be under-specified and so not yet well formed. His proposed 'product-centric frame for UX is a contribution to just such better formation. The contrast is with UX practitioners satisfied with their successful current practice and its framing, typically 'implement and test'. Identical overlap with the UX description is poor—just one descriptor. However, a large number of additional descriptors are identified. Many have subordinate relations with the initial UX description.

4.5   Sinclair Source Material (2023)

Summary

Sinclair's source material is 'current UX', that is ongoing. It reports a UX project. Nevertheless, the latter implicates a position on UX in general. Hence, its inclusion here. It comprises sections on—UX and Sitemap Reconciliation.

4.5.1   UX

Sinclair's take on UX is well expressed by the following quote:
  'I love UX *Design*, data, making things and then making them better. I'm lucky that I do UX. I love the simplicity of the idea at its core—*Test and Iterate*.
  I've been doing this for the past 20 years for more organisations than you can shake a stick at…. Everywhere I have been, as a Head of UX, I have set up a lab. This is the easiest and most effective way to get a design mind-set into an organisation and build *Client Trust* in a **User Experience Solution** (1.5.2). And the most creative part of the **User Experience** (1.3.2) design process happens when you put **Users** (1.1.2) in front of a product. The friction between the product and the User (1.1.2) is where novel solution(s) emerge…'

Guide Notes

UX *Design*, as a descriptor, is either a concept, as here in 'design, data' or a qualifier, as in 'design mind-set' and by implication 'design solution'. *Design* is the superordinate to UX Design Representation (2.1.2). The same for User Experience Problem (1.5.2). User

Experience Solution (1.5.2), however, is an identical concept. The need to distinguish UX, as design from UX, as User Experience (1.3.2) is noted. It is addressed at greater length later (13.2.1). It is a source of much misunderstanding between UX practitioners and so a key issue for the guide.

UX stands for User Experience (1.3.2).

Test and Iterate is one methodological approach to conducting UX design (2.1.2). The contrast is with *Specify then Implement* (3.1.2.3.3).

Client Trust could refer to the end-user or to the organisation commissioning the UX design—the more plausible interpretation. Its object is the User Experience Solution (1.5.2) of an implied User Experience Problem (1.5.2).

User Experience Solution (1.5.2) resolves a User Experience Problem (1.5.2).

User Experience (1.1.3) describes the Conscious Events (1.3.2) or Knowledge and Skills (1.3.2) experienced by the User (1.1.2).

User (1.1.2) describes someone who uses Human–Computer Technology (1.1.2) to do something as intended.

4.5.2   Sitemap Reconciliation

Perspective on UX is exposed in more detail by means of a project. Sinclair was asked by a major supplier to improve the User Experience (1.1.3) for domestic appliances.

According to Sinclair, 'This entailed reconciling two *Sitemaps*, one from the product team and one from other specialists. The process involved creating new pages to house search engine content and refining existing page types to improve *Engagement* and the *User Journey*. Finally taking a product finder from one national site and refactoring it for another. The work delivered the following *Assets* - a new *Sitemap*, a *Prototype* and a *Virtual Assistant*, tested with Users (1.1.1) in laboratory-based sessions.'

Guide Notes

UX, as a descriptor, stands for User Experience (1.2.2).

User Experience (1.2.2) is the primary descriptor of the initial UX description. The desired improvement here concerns the increased online sales of domestic appliances, such as refrigerators and pots and pans.

Sitemaps constitute the documentation of, and support for, user journeys. They are part of UX Practice (2.2.2).

Engagement describes a type of User Experience (1.1.3). It relates to the commitment of the User (1.1.1) to the task in hand. For example, in the case of this project to the purchase of domestic appliances.

User Journey describes how the User (1.1.1) navigates the site to achieve their goals, in this case the purchase of domestic appliances. For example, they may explore the site initially to gather general information on refrigerators, because their own has broken down and cannot be repaired. The User (1.1.1) may then go on to explore, in detail and at length, refrigerators within their budget, space and delivery requirements. Last, they may add the refrigerator to their trolley and finally activate the Buy Now Button.

Assets describe the outputs of the UX *Design Process*. In this case, they are a new *Sitemap*, a *Prototype* and a *Virtual Assistant*.

Identical Descriptors

User Experience Solution (1.5.2)/User Experience (1.1.3)/User (1.1.1).

Additional Descriptors

UXDesign/UX/Test-and-Iterate/ClientTrust/Sitemap/Engagement/User   Journey/Assets/ Virtual Assistant/User Journey/UX Design.

Review

Sinclair's position, concerning UX in general, is that current UX formation works for him. He has been a successful UX practitioner with many organisations. He imputes his success to his UX design practice. This comprises design, test and iterate. Also including the laboratory testing of users and the creation of a design mind-set to establish client trust. His innate modesty precludes mention of the contribution of his own natural creativity as a designer to this success. An outstanding creativity already apparent in his MSc project.

The UX description overlaps Sinclair's contribution with three descriptors. The absence of reference to the higher levels of description of general problem and specific scope could be made good as related to design and 'humans interacting with technology to do something as intended'. Likewise, for the lower level description of research as the 'acquisition and validation of implicit and explicit knowledge to support design'.

4.6   Timmer Source Material (2010)

Summary

Timmer's contribution is 'current UX', that is ongoing. He considers UX to be a field with origins in HCI, but which has fragmented in the process of its development. The source material comprises sections on—UX and its relation to Marketing, Advertising and Budgets/Sales.

4.6.1   UX

According to Timmer, 'UX is a *Field*, which has grown and fragmented. For example, *HCI* (*Human–Computer Interaction*) **Users** (1.1.2) have now become *Humans* and *Customers*.

UCD (*User-Centred Design*) has now become *HCD* (*Human-Centred Design*) and/or CCD (*Customer-Centred Design*). In addition, UX (**User Experience** 1.3.2) has become *HX* (*Human Experience*) and/or *CX* (*Customer Experience*).'

Guide Notes

UX, as a descriptor, stands for User Experience (1.3.2).

Field describes UX as a whole. As such, it is an alternative to UX Movement (1.4.2) and UX Community.

HCI (*Human–Computer Interaction*) now includes both humans and customers. The former is the superordinate. The latter implicates both the buying of objects and services as in ecommerce.

Users (1.1.2), consistent with *HCI*, have become *humans* and *customers*. The former is superordinate. The latter implicates the buying of both objects and services as in ecommerce.

UCD (*User-Centred Design*) has now become *HCD* (*Human-Centred Design*) and/or *CCD* (*Customer-Centred Design*). This is consistent with *HCI* earlier.

User Experience (1.3.2) is primary for the UX initial description.

HX and *CX* are alternatives to UX—*see earlier*.

4.6.2   Marketing and UX

'Further, the world of *Marketing* acts as if it owns these terms, applying them to anything and everything. Much of the UX/*HX*/*CX* commercial conference circuit these days comprises *Approaches* propagated by industry *Best-Practice*…

Business services are delivered by '*Channels*'. These, in turn, are maintained by Businesses for the purpose of contact and communication with *Consumers*. Door-to-door sales representatives, direct mail catalogues, a branch network of shops, call-centres and digital Website*s* are all *Channels* for managing contact with *Consumers*. *Channels* come with associated *Financial Expenses* to the *Business*. At the very least, for the maintenance of the *Channel*.'

Guide Notes

Marketing, as a descriptor, denotes the manner in which sales are organised in ecommerce businesses. The contrast is with design and production. *Marketing* includes *Advertising*, *Budgets and Sales* and the distribution/storage of goods for sale.

UX/*HX*/*CX* are described earlier.

Best-Practice is usually understood as best commercial practice. The contrast is with academic or research practice. Practitioners (1.6.2) strive to create and to apply *Best-Practice*. However, agreement on exactly what constitutes *Best-Practice* is limited or non-existent.

Business describes a type of commercial organisation, for example, banks, supermarkets, garages and private hospitals. All offer different services. For example, banks lend money, supermarkets sell food, garages repair cars and private hospitals deliver healthcare.

Channels describe the different ways in which business services contact and communicate with their customers For example, personally, as door-to-door sales representatives or indirectly via call centres.

Consumers describes the Users (1.3.2) of business services. Their description, however, varies with business type. For example, banks and supermarkets have customers, while hospitals have patients.

Channels, Consumers and *Business—see earlier.*

Financial Expenses describe the costs of running a *Business*, in general. Also, the costs of running a particular *Business*, such as *Marketing* or *Design*. Costs may be used as an alternative to *Expenses*. For planning and control purpose, they are formulated as budgets.

4.6.3 Advertising and UX

'*Sales* and *Marketing* functions within *Businesses* drive product sales to consumers across all relevant *Channels*. The latter use techniques such as advertising campaigns. It has always been difficult to measure the impact of a budgeted television commercial on sales within a particular *Channel*. However, in the case of *Digital Marketing*, this has proved to be relatively easy. A television advert rarely mentions a particular store. This to the detriment of the product or brand being advertised. However, in the case of the digital *Channel*, a *Banner Advert* can drive the prospective custome*r* directly to a retail ecommerce site. From thence, onwards to a *Purchasing Journey*.'

Guide Notes

Sales, as a descriptor denotes the transfer of ownership from seller to buyer. For example, beauty products from online retail ecommerce outlets to young consumer.

Marketing describes the manner in which sales are organised in ecommerce businesses. The contrast is with design and production. *Marketing* includes *Advertising*, *Budgets* and *Sales* and the distribution/storage of goods for sale.

Businesses, as a descriptor, denotes a type of commercial organisation, for example, banks, supermarkets, garages and private hospitals. All offer services, but of different kinds. For example, banks lend money, supermarkets sell food, garages repair cars and private hospitals deliver healthcare.

Channels describe the different ways in which business services contact and communicate with their customers For example, personally, as door-to-door sales representatives or indirectly via call centres.

Digital Marketing, as a descriptor, contrasts with offline promotion of goods and services.

Banner Advert describes a type of digital advert, which might target a specific group of customers, for example, pet food for dog owners.

Customers much like consumers describe the Users (1.3.2) of business services. Their description, however, varies with business type. For example, banks and supermarkets have customers, while hospitals have patients.

Purchasing Journey, as a descriptor denotes the website pages a customer needs to navigate in order to buy a desired product. Such pages might include brand information, category detail and product detail pages, along with other tangible content pages.

4.6.4   Budgets and Sales and UX

'One consequence of the directness of this relationship between digital advertising and digital purchasing, is that all *Budgets* can be measured within the *Business*. The expense of a banner advertising campaign, combined with the expenses of designing, building and maintaining a retail website for the digital *Channel*, can be identified. The cost can then be weighed against the direct contribution to sales of the digital *Channel. Business* expenses can be measured end-to-end. Thus, incremental sales from the digital channel, and so *Profits*, are known. The digital channel has a 'bright future' because of this accountability between the marketing expense of the channel, and the channel's marginal contribution to product sales.

In conclusion, this bright future for the design of 'effective' digital websites prompts consideration how the UX for the digital *Channel* might be structured for the purpose. Commercial practice is examined, in terms of the analysis tools available to the information architect. With the support of the former, practitioners design the core goal-oriented journeys (education, consideration and fulfilment). These along with interactive UX, such as navigation, that an effective website needs to support.'

Guide Notes

Budget, as a descriptor, denotes the financial investment, assigned to any particular purpose. For example, to fund a business service, such as manufacturing or an instance of such a service, such as advertising campaign. A comparable term is costs.

Business describes a type of commercial organisation, for example, banks, supermarkets, garages and private hospitals. All offer different services. For example, banks lend money, supermarkets sell food, garages repair cars and private hospitals deliver healthcare.

Channels denote the different ways in which business services contact and communicate with their customers For example, personally, as door-to-door sales representatives or indirectly via call centres.

Profits describe the difference between the costs/expenses of a *Product* or *Business Service* and the financial return accruing to them.

UX stands for User Experience (1.2.2).

Channels/UX—see earlier.

Identical Descriptors

User (1.1.1)/User Experience (1.1.3).

Additional Descriptors

UX/Field/HCI/UCD/UXHXCX/Marketing/Best-Practice/Business/Channel/Consumer/
Financial Expenses/Sales/Digital Marketing/Banner Advert/Customer/Purchasing Journey.

Review

Timmer's position on UX in general is that it is field, which has grown from its origins
in HCI and has fragmented in the process. His contribution shows how the fragments of
marketing, advertising and budgets/sales can be put together. UX, then, is continuous in
its development from HCI. It is also open to similar treatment and so to much the same
kind of formation.

   Timmer's contribution fits the UX initial description only modestly—two descriptors.
The absence of reference to the higher levels of description of general problem (1.6.2)
and particular scope (1.8.2) could be made good as related to UX design practice (1.11).
Likewise, for the lower-level descriptions of research (2.6) as the 'acquisition and validation of implicit and explicit knowledge to support design'. Also to 'humans interacting
with technology to do something as intended'.

4.7   Blyth Source Material (2023)

Summary

Blyth's contribution is 'post-UX'. After describing current UX, he goes on to propose
a novel characterisation of UX. It includes the concepts of Odyssey and Quality. It
constitutes a potential successor to UX, as currently understood and practised.

4.7.1   Conceptual Odyssey

'Anyone that recognises the portrait above (see 8.2 for the latter) will then surely recognise
at least parts of the *Conceptual Odyssey* that I will now trace out. As a *Community*, as an
Industry, and as *Individuals*, in the last twenty years we have journeyed from the primacy
of '*Usability*' to **User Experience** (1.3.2).

   The journey has been well documented and has had many heroes. There have been
triumphs and successes. UX has earned its place at the table in Powerful Organisations.

Many of those same **Practitioners** (1.6.2) now believe in the *Precepts* of UX as fervently as they did *Usability*.

But this journey has also given rise to many challenges and ordeals. A variety of distractions and inspirations in those two decades have encouraged Practitioners (1.3.1) to travel yet further, past UX as it is usually understood, and into new realms that have coloured differently again everything they were so confident of once before.

Novel project work, different *Industry Verticals*, **Professional** (Change and) **Development** (1.4.2), a spirited mentor or an inspiring junior team member. Each of these moments has the potential to change how one sees the world, and how one sees their work as a UX Practitioner (1.6.2).

Here I will consider a number of these inspirations—*Muses*, if you will—as a way to define and challenge 'what UX is'. As the *Journey* unfolds, we will start to consider UX as a subset in the wider notion of *Quality*.'

Guide Notes

Conceptual Odyssey, as a descriptor, denotes the contributor's personal UX Practitioner (1.6.2) journey. In the manner of Homer, but conceptual. The transposition of 'journey' from user to UX practitioner is novel. The temptation seems overwhelming, although no doubt simple association plays a role. Given the conceptual nature of the *Odyssey*, a comparable implementation nature cannot be far behind. Maybe in the form of UX *Precepts*—see later. The relation between the conceptual and implementation nature of the *Odyssey* is particularly interesting, as concerns the address of explicit and implicit UX Knowledge (2.6).

Community/Industry/Individuals describe different ways and levels in which UX Practitioners (1.6.2) can be partitioned. Characterisation of the latter implicates important aspects of their UX Practice (2.2.2) and the associated stakeholders—seniors, managers and Practitioners (1.6.2)—junior and senior.

Usability describes a UCD criterion of Performance (2.3.1). It also provides an overall contrast with Experience (1.3.2), as a general characterisation of a Movement (1.4.2)/ discipline.

User Experience (1.6.2), denotes the personal Experience of a user, brought about or not by the intentional UX Practice (2.2.2) of the UX Practitioner (1.6.2).

UX stands for User Experience (1.6.2).

Practitioner (1.6.2) describes the practising UX designer. The description makes clear that Practitioners (1.6.2) are leading UX. Certainly not academics or management, although both exert some influence.

Precepts, as descriptors, are neither clearly defined nor exemplified. They presumably apply to 'best-practice' of some kind. Better specification would help with the explicit/implicit design knowledge distinction. It would also help to clarify its relationship with the artistic inspiration of the *Muses*. Further, with the proper goals of UX research.

Professional (Change and) Development (1.4.2), as a descriptor, denotes career progress or advancement. For example from junior to senior or from novice to experienced. It also denotes the changes, which the UX Movement (1.4.2) seeks to advance.

Muse describes a source of artistic inspiration. In this case, it is Blyth's personal and conceptual artistic inspiration. The latter informs his UX Practitioner (1.6.2) *Journey*. The idea that UX and its associated UX Practice (2.3.2) are informed by inspiration and artistic inspiration, at that, is certainly novel. It goes beyond *UX*, as currently conceived and practised. This is a claim made by Blyth himself. Interestingly, it opens up a new way for UX to advance.

Quality, as a descriptor, seems to be a new UX application of the term. It includes UX as a possible subset. Little more is disclosed here.

Identical Descriptors

User Experience (1.1.3)/Practitioners (1.3.1)/Professional (Change and) Development (1.2.3).

Additional Descriptors

Conceptual Odyssey/Community, Industry/Individuals/Usability/Individuals/Precepts/ Journey/Usability/Muse/Quality.

Review

Blyth's position on UX in general is that it is in need of serious reconstruction—from its fundamental concepts to its professional organisation. To that end, he proposes such a reconstruction. It includes novel concepts, such as 'odyssey' and 'quality'. It also includes the novel organisation of a UX practitioner 'community'. It constitutes a potential successor to UX, as currently understood and practised.

There is overlap with the initial UX description—three descriptors. Many descriptors are at a lower level than those of the initial description and so could constitute subordinates of some of its concepts.

Chapter Review

The practitioner UX source material contributions are presented, as they describe UX in general. The initial UX description is applied to the source material, as part of the process of constructing a final description. A majority of the contributions identify the origin of UX to be HCI. There is no surprise there. However, there is a wide range of positions as to how and to what extent current UX in general needs to be developed further—from very little to a complete reconstruction. As to the former, Sinclair considers UX in the form of his current practice to be fit-for-success-purpose, at least for him. As to the latter, Blyth considers UX to be in need of complete reconstruction. The remaining contributors argue for different forms and degrees of development. Grant considers UX as experience can be accommodated by UCD/HCI. Chakraborty considers UX should integrate business, markets and management with perceived utility in the manner of his 'product-centric' frame. Timmer considers the fragmented UX of marketing, advertising and budgets/sales need bringing together, as in his own proposal. This broad range of positions on UX in general lies at the centre of the lack of consensus, concerning UX in general. Hence, the need for the present guide.

Identical descriptor overlap is only modest between the initial UX description and the source materials. Many additional descriptors are identified. These tend to be at a lower level of description than those of the initial UX description and more specifically UX-related.

Chapter Carry Forward

The carry-forward from this chapter and Chaps. 5–10 appears in Appendix 1. It constitutes the basis for the initial UX description and hence for the guide to framing design practice for UX. The appendix is intended to support readers in applying the initial UX description to the UX practitioner source material. Also, in completing the associated exercise assignments. Appendix 1 is not for reading as a text in itself, but for consultation in its application.

4.8   Exercise Assignment

The exercise assignment is intended to test readers' understanding and application of the concepts presented. Also to support tailoring the initial UX description to their own design requirements.

Consulting 4.2–4.7

– *Check* the shared descriptors between the initial UX description and the UX source material.
– *Do you agree* with the descriptors identified? If not, then
– *Compile* your own list.
– *Justify* your listing.

– *Add* to the descriptor listing any changes, implied in or additional to, your completion of the Exercise Assignment 3.8.
– *How* do your changes add to the completeness, coherence and fitness-for-purpose of the descriptors?
– *Justify* your claims

– *Select* a UX paper of your own, of a colleague or of your supervisor.

Consulting 4.2–4.7.

- *Identify* in **Bold** descriptors identical to those of the initial UX description.
- *Identify* in *Italics* additional descriptors appearing in the paper.
- *Compare* the identical and additional descriptors identified with those identified here.
- *Note* the similarities.
- *Note* the differences.
- *Compare* similarities and the differences.
- *Assess* the comparison.
- *Reflect* and *Conclude* on the comparison.
- *Give* your reasons.

Reference

Polit, D., & Beck, C. (2010). Generalization in quantitative and qualitative research: Myths and strategies. *International Journal of Nursing Studies, 47*(11), 1451–1458.

UX Practitioner Source Material Describing UX Design Practice

5

5.1 Introduction

The chapter presents source material for UX design practice. The same guide summary/ review structure of 4.1 is used here. Likewise, for the concepts and their relations. To crosscheck the UX contributions with the initial UX descriptors, see Appendix 1.

5.2 Chakraborty Source Material (2023)

Summary

Chakraborty argues that pre-UX design practice was well-specified and essentially linear in nature. Current UX design practice, however, is less well specified and so, less linear. The lack of specification has resulted from the changes that the exponential growth in interactive technology have brought about, in particular the reshaping of people's lives.

5.2.1 UX Approaches

'The UX **Approaches** (3.1.2.2) of the late 90s, early 2000s to design **Practice** (2.2.1) were largely based on a *Linear Development Cycle*. Ideas are conceived, *Requirements* are gathered, *Designs* are built, and *Tests* are conducted. Eventually, the thing is launched and needs to be operated and maintained.'

© The Author(s), under exclusive license to Springer Nature Switzerland AG 2025   39
J. Long, *Guide to Framing Design Practice for UX*, Synthesis Lectures
on Human-Centered Informatics, https://doi.org/10.1007/978-3-031-68981-9_5

Guide Notes

Approaches, as descriptors, denote general ways in which people go about doing things, like addressing issues or solving problems. Here, they refer to UX. *Approaches* can be contrasted with UX Frameworks (3.1.2.1) being less formal [2].

Practice (2.2.1) describes what designers, among others, do. The contrast is with research.

Linear Development Cycle describes a particular way of configuring the design process—here ideas, *Requirements* and *Tests*. It is sometimes referred to as 'top down'. Linear cycles are typified by *Structured Analysis and Design Methods'* [2].

5.2.2   Growth of Technology

'Since the start of the 2000s, consider how the growth in technology has become exponential and reshaped every aspect of our lives. From *Mobility* to *Metaverse*, *Internet of Things* to *Augmented Reality*, the *World of Experience* has become rather too complicated. While UX has become essential, it inhabits an uncomfortable space, where it's tricky to define and problematic to own. The UX designer's role (assuming there is such a role in a company) is often confined to designing a few widgets for the web page.'

Guide Notes

Mobility, as a descriptor, supported by ubiquitous computing, denotes how people can remain in communication, wherever they are and whatever the time. The contrast is with a telephone landline message recorder.

Metaverse, supported by new synthesising technology, is a view of what many UX Practitioners (1.5.2) believe to be the next iteration of the Internet. It would share a single, immersive, persistent, *3D Virtual Space*. Here, humans would be able to experience a form of *Virtual Life*. The contrast is with experiencing life in the physical world.

Internet of Things supported by recent platform developments, denotes a network of physical objects or 'things'. The latter contain sensors, software, and other technologies for the purpose of connecting and exchanging data with other devices and systems over the Internet. Users (1.1.2) may also be connected to parts of this Internet. Examples of types of *Internet of Things* (usually termed 'smart') include mobile 'phones, domestic security and heating systems, refrigerators, door locks, fire alarms, watches, fitness trackers and so on. The latter, for example, in the form of a watch, can monitor a person's heart rate and blood pressure, while exercising. Also, initiate alarms, when danger limits are about to be exceeded. Further, to change the current exercise programme to one more appropriate. The contrast here is with a simple heart monitor, which can only display heart rate.

Augmented Reality, as a descriptor, supported by recent developments in virtual software, integrates digital information (the 'augmentation') with the User's (1.1.2) environment (the 'reality') in real time. An example would be a game, in which users look for 'targets' in their local neighbourhood. The targets might be animated characters, which pop up on their smart 'phone or tablet. User Experience (1.2.2) may be enhanced by such applications.

World of Experience, as a descriptor, is the set of Experiences (1.3.2), afforded by the types of new interactive technology referenced earlier. They identify the source material, which affirms the growth of technology and its effects on all aspects of people's lives.

Identical Descriptors

Approaches (3.1.2.2) Practice (2.2.1).

Additional Descriptors

Approaches/LinearDevelopmenCycle/Technology/Mobility/Metaverse/Internet of Things/ 3D Virtual Space/Virtual Life/Augmented Reality/World of Experience.

Review

Chakraborty claims that pre-UX design practice was well-specified and linear. Current UX design practice, however, is neither. He believes the changes have been brought about by the exponential growth in interactive technology.

Chakraborty's source material shares only two descriptors with the initial UX description. This is inspite of its obvious relevance to UX. Many of the concepts, however, are subordinate to those of the initial UX description. The difference in levels may be due to the source contribution, to the initial UX description or some combination of the two.

5.3   Cummaford Source Material (2022)

Summary

Cummaford presents UX design practice as 'best-practice'. Other aspects of best-practice are presented elsewhere (9.2 and 10.2).

5.3.1   Changes to Best-Practice (2.2.1)

'To the latter ends, the changes to Best-Practice since the completion of the research, are identified and implications for Best-Practice and for HCI engineering design problems application format noted. Future UX research would do well to take account of both sets of implications.'

Guide Notes

Best-Practice (2.2.1), as a descriptor, usually describes best commercial practice, as recognised and agreed, by experienced UX Practitioners (1.5.2). Here, it is subordinate to Practice (2.2.1), but superordinate to UX Practice (2.3.2).

UX, as a descriptor, stands for User Experience (1.2.2).

Cummaford's proposed changes to *Best*-Practice (2.2.1) as they relate to UX Practice (2.2.2) follow:

1. 'UX *Design* for **User Experience** (1.3.2).
2. *Design Methods*, enhanced by technical advances in Data Capture.
3. *Online Design Funnel Testing*.
4. *Online 'AB' Testing*.
5. *Lean* UX *Design Methods*.
6. *Minimum Viable Product (MVP)*.
7. *Atomic Design Methods*.
8. *Online 'Scaled Up' User Testing'*.

Guide Notes

UX *Design*, as a descriptor, implies the UX Practice (2.2.2) by which Practitioners (1.5.2) go about designing, also the product of designing.

User Experience (1.3.2) describes the desired result of UX designing.

Design Methods embody methodological or 'how' knowledge. The contrast is with declarative or 'what' knowledge.

Online Design Funnel Testing, as a descriptor, is subordinate to UX Practice (2.2.2) and UX Performance (2.2.2). It is a typical form of UX website testing.

Online 'AB' Testing is subordinate to UX Practice (2.2.2) and UX Performance (2.2.2). It is a typical form of UX website testing.

Lean UX *Design Methods* describe cut-down or basic methods. They are subordinate to UX Practice (2.2.2).

Minimum Viable Product (MVP) is comparable to a design solution. It is a much-used term in UX design. *MVP is* subordinate to UX Practice (2.2.2) and UX Performance (2.2.2).

Atomic Design Methods are constituted of basic design 'elements'. Such methods are subordinate to UX Practice (2.2.2).

'Scaled Up' User Testing is in contrast to individual, off-line, face-to-face testing, for example, by interview. It is subordinate to UX Practice (2.2.2)/Practice (2.2.1) and to Performance (2.2.1).

Identical Descriptors

Practice (2.2.1)/User Experience (1.3.2).

Additional Descriptors

Best-Practice/Design Methods/Online Transaction Testing/Online Funnel Testing/Online AB Testing/Atomic Design Methods/Lean UX Design Methods/Minimum Viable Product (MVP)/*Online Scaled Up User Testing'*.

Review

Cummaford's contribution comprises a list of requirements for UX design practice, as 'best-practice. Although the list itself is complete, the items on the list are not detailed. Cummaford's source material has only a modest two descriptor overlap with the initial UX description. This is inspite of it being the topic of the contribution. This may be due to the technical content of the latter or to the level of the initial UX description. There are many additional and relational associations of the subordinate/superordinate type.

5.4 Grant Source Material (2023)

Summary

Grant's contribution to UX design practice comprises sections on UCD Practice and Evaluation. It is primarily contrastive, but of interest in spite of not using the term UX. Importantly, UCD also claims to design for user experiences other than usability.

5.4.1 UCD Practice

'Grant's *UCD* **Practice** (2.2.1) is 'varied'. Some project*s* focusing on Physical and Software Ergonomics separately, but others together. For example, a project procuring software systems from different suppliers. The systems needed to be physically integrated onto the desks in a control room. The analysis also included the **User Experience** (1.3.2) of wider systems, paperwork, procedures, and so forth.

Practice (2.2.1) is evidence-based. Recommendations draw on literature from *Ergonomics, Human Factors*, HCI, etc. Recommendations are also mapped back to the relevant standards clauses. The latter involve extensive reading, trawling through the literature. Findings are collated into an Excel-based *Commonplace Book*. Key insights are captured from research *Standards, Guidance*, etc. Before keeping such a book, it was necessary to search for repeated problems from scratch. The commonplace book supports greater efficiency.

Analysis is creative. For example, spreadsheets to find different patterns in the data, collected about systems. Also combining analytical methods to create one, which is more robust. The latter supports better understanding of a given situation from many different angles, for example, the risk of *Use Errors*, associated with Interactive Interfaces.'

Guide Notes

UCD (User-Centred Design), as a descriptor, contrasts with Product-Centric Design and Experience-Centred Design (ECD).

Practice (2.2.1) describes the process of *User-Centred Design*, which in turn describes its product. *UCD Practice* is subordinate to Practice (2.2.1). It can be at a higher, lower or at the same level of description as UX Design Practice (2.3.2).

User Experience (1.3.2) equates to UX, when used to describe what a User (1.1.2) experiences.

Practice (2.2.1)—see earlier.

Standards can be either explicit and public or organisational standards, as here. Alternatively, standards might informally indicate the quality of work, expected from a designer or a design team. The former characterise *UCD*, but, at least so far, not UX. It remains to be seen, if such developments take place. UX Practitioners (1.6.2) are divided on the matter.

Guidance can be treated much as *Standards* and *Research Standards* earlier. *Guidance*, however, in contrast can be quite varied and its status much less clear. Such *Guidance* might include—published papers in academic journals, papers from the professional UX conference circuit, organisation memos. Also, other prescriptions, for example for 'best-practice' and associated templates. *Guidance* from more experienced designers and Practitioners (1.6.2) is, of course, also common.

Use Errors are much the same as errors or user errors. The implication is that Users (1.1.2) are involved in some way or other. The contrast is with software or system errors. The descriptor is subordinate to Performance (2.2.1).

5.4.2   Evaluation

'As concerns Evaluation, *Tried-and-Tested Methods* are applied. For example, in the case of quantifiable *Subjective User Data*, the System Usability Scale and the Single Ease Question. Both are claimed to have been validated by research. However, questionnaires are developed, if none suitable are available…. The contributor concludes that particular Practices (2.2.1) are usually a mixture and depend on the project. For example, *Projects* with greater uncertainty use more *Trial and Error Practice* to work through the assumptions.'

Guide Notes

Tried and Tested Methods describe methodological knowledge to support design. The contrast is with untried and untested methods. Such as those developed by Practitioners (1.5.2) themselves (other than with respect to their own experience).

Subjective User Data describe user-generated data, for example, concerning some aspects of usability or Experience (1.3.2). The contrast is with objective data, for example, time-on-task, as measured by the computer.

Practices (2.2.1) contrasts with design knowledge.

Trial and Error Practice describes a type of design Practice (2.2.1) which is also known as 'implement and test'. The contrast is with 'specify then implement'. Both design Practices (2.2.1) are at the same level of description and design is superordinate to both.

Identical Descriptors

User Experience (1.3.2)/Practice (2.2.1).

Additional Descriptors

UCD/Practice/User Experience/Ergonomics/Human Factors/Commonplace Book/Standards/Guidance/Use Errors/Tried-and-Tested Methods/Subjective User Data/Projects.

Review

Grant applies a range of UCD practice and evaluation methods in his design practice. It addresses user experiences in addition to usability.

Only two descriptors are shared between Grant's source material and the initial UX description. Many of the concepts, however, have both subordinate and superordinate relations. Due, perhaps, to the source contribution, to the initial UX description or some combination.

5.5   Sinclair Source Material (2023)

Summary

Sinclair's contribution to UX design practice is in the form of a project report. Its length precludes complete inclusion. However, extracts suffice to characterise his UX design practice. Its sections comprise—Usability Study, Sample and Equipment, Sessions, Prototype Testing, Prototype, Tree Test, Product Category Detail, Search Landing Page, Buy Now-Call to Action, Product Detail Page, Results Iteration 1 and Results Iteration 2 and 3.

5.5.1   Usability Study

'… 15 participants were recruited for a lab-based *Usability Study*.'

Guide Note

Usability Study, as a descriptor, is intended to increase the online sales of domestic appliances. It is subordinate to UX Practice (2.2.2) and to UX Performance (2.2.2).

5.5.2 Sample and Equipment

'With respect to the *Sample* and *Equipment*, the Participants were from BC1 and had purchased a domestic appliance within the last three years. Lab equipment included— Desktop Windows Mid range tower + screen.'

Guide Notes

Sample describes the actual number, as opposed to the possible number of participants taking part in the *Usability Study*.

    Equipment describes the tools used in the conduct of the *Usability Study*. *Equipment* is subordinate to UX Practice (2.2.2).

5.5.3 Sessions

'Concerning *Sessions*, each had a facilitator and a note taker. The *Sessions* ran for 1 hour and were divided into three parts—an open-ended interview, prototype testing and a *Tree Test*. In addition, there was an interview. The interview was recorded.'

Guide Notes

Sessions describe the units of testing, usually in terms of duration and type. The latter depend on the nature and purpose of the testing.

Tree Test evaluates specific aspects of an actual or possible Internet site. The contrast is with *Interview*.

5.5.4 Prototype Testing

'The *Prototype Testing* lasted 25–30 min. Areas and content not covered by the participant's free exploration were prompted or *Walked Through*.'

Guide Notes

Prototype Testing describes the early testing of designs, before they have been finalised and released.

    Walk Through is a type of test, for example for usability or for User Experience (1.3.2). The testee usually talks their way through the design without actually completing the tasks. The user reflections are intended to provide insights into the appropriateness of the design.

5.5.5 Prototype

'Its primary functions were to accommodate the new *Sitemap*. The summary findings of the *Project* (each based on 3 iterations) follow.'

Guide Notes

Prototype constitutes a particular prototype format. It is subordinate to UX Design Representation (2.1.2).

Sitemap is the object of the redesign. It is subordinate to UX Design Representation (2.1.2).

5.5.6 Product Category Detail

'Concerning *Product Category Detail (PCD)*

– A number of participants would not scroll down the page.
– Images were hugely important to grab participants' attention and identify the content.
– All search category items were linked to the relevant new *SLPs*.'

Product Category Detail (PCD) describes, *Domestic Appliances* and refrigerators. *PCD* is subordinate to UX Representation (2.1.2).

SLP—see following.

5.5.7 Search Landing Page

'As concerns *Search Landing Page (SLP)*

– Most participants did not interact with feature benefits, when they were presented in a carousel.'

Guide Notes

Search Landing Page (SLP) categorises a type of Internet page.

5.5.8 Buy Now-Call to Action

'The *Buy Now-Call to Action (CTA)* was off-putting to a number of participants, as they were in a research mode and not ready to purchase.'

Buy Now-Call to Action is an example of, and subordinate to, UX Representation (2.1.2).

5.5.9 Product Detail Page

'With respect to the *Product Detail Page (PDP)*

- Participants responded well to 'How it stacks up'.
- Most participants tended to focus on the product specification.
- As concerns navigation, creating a series of pages the user could identify and navigate was a challenge.'

Guide Notes

Product Detail Page complements the *Product Category Detail (PCD)* page. The descriptor is an example of, and subordinate to, UX Representation (2.1.2).

5.5.9.1 Results—Iteration 1
'These Results are acceptable, but disappointing as the minimum requirement is to ensure that **Users** (1.1.2) are aware of the options available to them.

Iterations 2 and 3

- With the second iteration, the Results were still the main focus on the *Desktop*. On *Mobile* and *Tablet*, most participants focused on the questions and used the Next and Previous buttons to move between choices.
- The third iteration removed the results and provided a clear *Call to Action* at the end of the questions.
- Difficulty remained in the clarity of *Feedback* showing selected choices, and the affordance given to deselect.'

Guide Note

Feedback, as a descriptor denotes the information provided to a participant on the performance of a task after an associated input.

Identical Descriptors

Users (1.1.2).

Additional Descriptors

Usability Study/Sample/Equipment/Sessions/Tree Test/Prototype Testing/Walk Through/ Prototype/Sitemap/Product Category Detail Page/Search Landing Page/Buy Now-Call to Action/Product Detail Page/Feedback/Desktop/Tablet/Mobile.

Review

Sinclair describes in detail the UX design practice, which he applied in a particular project. It is both explicit and highly attuned to Internet design.

Sinclair's source material has a single identity overlap with the initial UX description. This is in spite of the work being a clear example of UX design practice. There are, however, many relations at a lower level of description. For example, between 'search landing page (SLP) and UX representation. This may be due to the domain specific nature of the work (Internet site redesign), insufficient higher-level source contribution concepts or UX descriptors being at a lower-level.

5.6 Timmer Source Material (2010)

Summary

Timmer's source material sections comprise—Conversion Funnel, Statistical Feature, Business Website and Analytics Data. A detailed analysis of each is offered in the context of UX design practice.

5.6.1 Conversion Funnel

'The source material contribution opens with the concept of the *Conversion Funnel*. The latter has its origins in *Website Analytics*. It speaks to a **User**'s *(1.1.2) Journey* across web pages leading to the achievement of a business service goal. For example, a sale, the booking of an appointment, or the completion of an application form. In the retail context, the latter involves clicking on a *Checkout* button. The user is then guided through a stepwise process, to buy the product. This involves steps such as *Personal Details* (needed for shipping and logistics); *Financial Details* (needed for billing and finance); *Accept Terms and Conditions* (needed for legal reasons); *Opt-In* (to future product marketing updates and offers), and so forth. Each of these sub-sets of customer data is mandated by the business, for service delivery in the digital channel.'

Guide Notes

Conversion Funnel, as a descriptor, denotes a User's (1.1.2) navigation towards, and possible achievement of, a goal. It is a common device of UX Internet design. It is the object of UX *Design Practice* and subordinate to it.

Website Analytics are statistical ways of treating data associated with *User Journeys* (see next note).

User's Journey describes their navigation through Internet *Pages* to achieve some goal. It is the object of UX Practice (2.2.2) and subordinate thereto.

Checkout denotes a buyer's decision to complete a purchase. *Checkout* precedes payment.

Personal Details typically include at least the name and the address of the potential customer. The details are required to complete the transaction and effect the delivery of items purchased.

Financial Details

Typically include bank account or credit card details. These are required to effect payment to complete the transaction associated with a sale.

Accept Terms and Conditions include those required by the business effecting the transaction. In principle, they should be read and understood by the latter is rarely the case. Problems may ensue.

5.6.2 Statistical Feature

'A statistical feature of such step-wise journeys is that there cannot be more Users (1.1.2) at Step 3 than at Step 1. The *Conversion Funnel* can only loose Users (1.1.2) and subsequent service opportunities. *Website Analytics* enable each page on the *User's Journey* to receive a unique '*Tag*'. As a result, user clicks can be tracked. Buttons and controls on all pages can be tagged. If there is more than one way between two steps, individual buttons on the page can be assessed for how well they guide the *User's Journey*. *Web Analytics* claim that this tagging and analysis process informs Website optimisation. This is done by generating statistical aggregations of user behaviour on a set of tagged pages.

For example, Fig. 5.1 shows data from an illustrative *Conversion Funnel* for a *Quote and Buy Service*, offered by a business on the *Digital Channel*. A five-page journey is the object of design. However, although all pages are tagged, a *Conversion Funnel* has been set-up for a *User Journey* from offering a quotation, to purchase confirmation. That is, the last four pages of the journey.

Guide Notes

Users (1.1.2) are superordinate to *Customers* and *Consumers*. They use Human–Computer Technology (1.3.2) to conduct transactions.

Conversion Funnel/Website Analytics/User's Journey—see earlier.

Tag is a unique page marker by which a *User's Journey* can be followed in detail page by page.

	Pet Insurance Product Page	Quote £ 9.00	Personal Details Form	Review Order	Confirmation Thank you
	Get a quote	Buy now	Next	Confirm	Continue shopping
Visitors	832	261	38	12	10
% retained from last step		31.3%	14.6%	31.6%	83.3%
Conversion funnel rate		100%	14.6%	4.6%	**3.8%**

Fig. 5.1 Conversion funnel

Quote and Buy Service indicates the price of an ecommerce product and the way in which it can be purchased.

Digital Channel is in contrast to an equivalent off-line means, for communicating with customers about sales of products and services.

5.6.3 Business Website

'On a business web site, a Pet Insurance *Product* is described. It is offered for purchase in the *Digital Channel*. *Product* information is displayed to the user on a single page. This Pet Insurance *Product Page* is shown in Fig. 5.1 top left. *Analytics data* reveal that on a single day, the *Product Page* had 832 unique visitors. The page holds an important primary *Call to Action* in *Get a Quote*.

When the user clicks *Get a Quote*, on the *Product Page*, they are taken to a *Quote Page*. Accurate quotations require information to be elicited from the prospective customer. So, the *Quote Page* radio buttons and drop-down choice controls support a description of the pet to be insured. A dynamic quote is thereby generated within the page, based on the *User's* actions. Here, a quote of £9.00 results. Once a well-formed quotation is generated and displayed, a *Buy Now Button* is offered to the **User** (1.1.2). Analytics show 261 Users (1.1.2), of the 832 Users (1.1.2), who visited the *Product Page*, progressed to see the *Quote Page*. That is 31.3% retention of interest in the product. This group, of 261 Users (1.1.2), who click on the *Get a Quote Button*, may be considered by the business as a target of '*Warm Prospects*'. These are Users (1.1.2) judged as having a genuine interest in the product. They are ready to act within the *Digital Channel*. Of the 571 *Visitors* to the *Product Page* that did not seek a quote, some may have been conducting *Personal Research*. Later, they may progress an order via a call centre *Channel* or approached a shop Branch or broker channel. Note that the *Digital Channel* may still meet important user needs, even when action within the channel is not evident.

If the prospective customer then clicks the *Buy Now Button* on the *Quote Page*, having considered the quote, they are taken to a '*Personal Details*' form. There, *Contact Details* and *Financial Details* are captured. A *Next Button* then progresses the *User* onto a *Review Order Page*. Next, a *Confirm Button* generates an *Order Confirmation Page*. In principle, everybody who sees the *Order Confirmation Page* is a *Customer* of the *Business*. They have bought the product via the *Digital Channel*. The *Order Confirmation Page* is thus the end of a *Transaction Process*. It cannot be refound and visited via the navigation, or passed as a *URL* (*Uniform Resource Locator*) within an email.'

Guide Notes

Pages, such as—*Product Page, Quote Page, Review Order Page,* and *Order Confirmation Page* are all types of web *page,* whose meaning is obvious from the text.

   Buttons, such as—*Get a Quote, Buy Now Button, Get a Quote Button, Buy Now Button, Next Button* and *Confirm Button* are all types of *Buttons,* whose meaning is obvious from the text.

   Warm Prospects are potential *Customers,* showing an interest in a product.

   Digital Channel is in contrast to an equivalent off-line means, for communicating with customers about sales of products and services.

   Visitors have selected a web page for a particular purpose, which may or may not be known or inferred.

   Channels, such as Digital Channel, Call Centre Channel and Broker Channel, as descriptors, are all types of *Channels,* whose meaning is obvious from the text. They are all accessible via the *Digital Channel.*

   Digital Channel—see earlier.

   Personal Details typically include at least the name and the address of the potential customer. The details are required to complete the transaction and effect the delivery of items purchased.

   Accept Terms and Conditions include those required by the business effecting the transaction. In principle, they should be read and understood by the latter is rarely the case. Problems may ensue.

   Contact Details typically include name and address, mobile number and email. Also, other details, which may be required by the *Business* to effect a transaction and a delivery.

Financial Details

Typically include bank account or credit card details. These are required to effect payment to complete the transaction associated with a sale.

   Digital Channel—see earlier.

   Transaction Process describes the behaviours required to effect the sales of goods and services.

   URL (*Uniform Resource Locator*) is a unique identifier serving to locate an Internet resource. It is also called a web address. URLs consist of parts—including protocol and domain names. The latter tell a web browser how and where to retrieve a resource.

5.6.4   Analytics Data

'*Analytics Data* show, across these pages, a gradual drop-off in *Visitor* numbers. Prospective customers 'bounce out' of this journey to purchase the product. Maybe via bookmarks or by closing the window. It can be seen that only 10 **Users** (1.1.2) saw the *Confirmation Page* on the day in question. Ten prospective *Customers* became actual customers of the *Business*. In Fig. 5.1, percentage statistics are tabulated below the *Analytics Data* for page visits. These reflect the number of *Visitors* retained by the *Digital Channel*, from preceding steps. Only 14.6% of people who sought a quote, elected to *Buy Now*. Of this group, two-thirds were then lost during form filling.

Finally, a *Conversion Funnel* has been set up from the *Quote Page* through to the *Confirmation Page*. If the 261 *Visitors* to the *Quote Page* are considered a target group for purchasing (the *Warm Prospects*). And if only 10 of that group of prospective customers actually became customers (the ones that saw the *Confirmation Page*). Then, the 'business' *Digital Channel* has a 3.8% *Conversion Rate* for the product.'

Guide Notes

Analytics Data describe statistical results of treating data associated with *User Journeys* (see next note).

Visitors have selected a web *Page* as part of their *Journey*, which may or may not be known or inferred.

Users *(1.1.2)* denote people interacting with Human–Computer Technology (1.1.2), as intended.

Confirmation Page denotes the User's (1.1.2) option for concluding a transaction.

Business describes an organisation, which conducts transactions.

Digital Channel is in contrast to an equivalent off-line means, for communicating with customers about sales of products and services.

Buy Now offers the User (1.1.2) the option of completing a transaction.

Conversion Funnel describes a User's (1.1.2) navigation towards, and possible achievement of, a goal.

Quote Page denotes the offered cost price of an object or service.

Confirmation Page/Visitors/Quote Page—see earlier.

Warm Prospects denotes interested *Prospective Customers*.

Confirmation, Buy Now, Digital Channel, Quote Pages Page/Business/Digital Channel—see earlier.

Conversion Rate describes the ratio or percentage of users navigating from a *Quote Page* for the cost of a *Product* or a service to the *Confirmation Page*. The navigation, in effect, completes the sale or subscription.

Identical Descriptors

User (1.1.2).

Additional Descriptors

Customers/Consumers/Conversion	Funnel/Analytics	Data/User	Journey/Business/
Checkout/Personal Details/Financial Details/Accept Terms and Conditions/Users/Tag/
Pages/Personal Details/Quote Page/Buy Now/Accept Terms and Conditions/Warm
Prospects/Confirmation Page/Website Analytics/Buttons/Quote and Buy Service/Digital
Channel/Pages/Visitors/Customers/Transaction Process/Conversion Rate.

Review

Timmer presents an in-depth analysis of the descriptors involved in UX design practice.
The details expose the complexities of such practice.

Timmer's source material has only a single overlap with the initial UX description.
However, the work is a good example of UX design practice. Many relations, however, are identified at a lower level of description. For example, between pages and UX
design representation. This may be due to limited higher-level source contribution concepts. Alternatively, to poverty of UX space descriptor lower-level concepts. Last, the
relations may be due to some admixture of these possible reasons. Other contributions
may be informative on the matter.

Chapter Review

The practitioner source material contributions are presented, as they describe UX design
practice. The initial UX design practice description is applied to the source material, as part
of the process of constructing a final description. Although all the contributions address
UX, they do so in very different ways. Chakraborty analyses the effects of the exponential
growth of interactive technology and its reshaping of people's lives on UX design practice. Cummaford proposes a list of requirements for UX design as 'best-practice'. Grant
presents the range of UCD practice and evaluation methods, used in his own design practice. They address user experiences in addition to usability. Sinclair describes in detail the
UX design practice, which he successfully applied in a particular project. It is both explicit
and highly attuned to Internet design. Last, Timmer presents an in-depth analysis of the
descriptors involved in UX design practice. The details expose the complexities of such
practice. Although there is some overlap between the different contributions on UX design
practice, the lack of agreement contributes to the lack of consensus, concerning UX design
practice and so the need for the present guide.

Identical descriptor overlap is only modest between the initial UX description and the
source materials. Many additional descriptors are identified. These tend to be at a lower
level of description than those of the initial description.

Chapter Carry Forward

The carry-forward from Chaps. 4–10 appears in Appendix 1. It constitutes the basis for the initial UX description and hence for the guide to framing design practice for UX. The appendix is intended to support readers in applying the initial UX description to the UX practitioner source material. Also, in completing the associated exercise assignments. Appendix 1 is not for reading as a text in itself, but for consultation in its application.

5.7 Exercise Assignment

The exercise assignment is intended to test readers' understanding and application of the concepts presented. Also to support tailoring the initial UX description to their own design requirements.

Consulting 6.2–6.7

- *Check* the shared descriptors between the initial UX description and the UX source material.
- *Do you agree* with the descriptors identified? If not, then
- *Compile* your own list.
- *Justify* your listing.

- *Add* to the descriptor identification listing any changes, implied in or additional to, your completion of the Exercise Assignment 3.8.
- *How* do your changes add to the completeness, coherence and fitness-for-purpose of the descriptors?
- *Justify* your claims

- *Select* a UX paper of your own, of a colleague or of your supervisor.

Consulting 6.2–6.7

- *Identify* in **Bold** descriptors identical to those of the initial UX description.
- *Identify* in *Italics* additional descriptors appearing in the paper.
- *Compare* the identical and additional descriptors identified with those identified here.
- *Note* the similarities.
- *Note* the differences.
- *Compare* similarities and the differences.
- *Assess* the comparison.
- *Reflect* and *Conclude* on the comparison.
- *Give* your reasons.

5.8   Note

[1] For an extended address of the difference between Framework and Approach, as concerns their formality, see Long (2021).

Reference

Long, J. (2021). *Approaches and frameworks for HCI research.* Cambridge University Press.

UX Practitioner Source Material Describing Framing UX Design Practice

6

6.1 Introduction

The chapter presents source material for framing UX design practice. The same guide summary/review structure of 4.1 is used here. Likewise for the concepts and their relations. To crosscheck the UX contributions with the initial UX descriptors, see Appendix 1.

6.2 Grant Source Material (2023)

Summary

Grant proposes a way of framing design practice. Its sections comprise—Context of Use, User Requirements and Design Solutions. They derive from UCD/HCI. The contrast with UX is instructive.

6.2.1 Approach

'The contribution uses the steps from BS EN ISO 9241-210 as a broad **Approach** (3.1.2.2) for framing *Design Practice*. Most notably to understand the *Context of Use*, specify the *User Requirements*, produce Design Solutions, and evaluate the design until a fit-for-purpose solution is found. For each these steps, specific Approaches (3.1.2.2) that work are used.'

Guide Notes

Approach (3.1.2.2), as a descriptor, is superordinate to UX Design Practice (2.2.2).

© The Author(s), under exclusive license to Springer Nature Switzerland AG 2025   57
J. Long, *Guide to Framing Design Practice for UX*, Synthesis Lectures
on Human-Centered Informatics, https://doi.org/10.1007/978-3-031-68981-9_6

Design Practice (2.2.2) is subordinate to Practice (3.3.1).

Practice relates to the practical design activities of Practitioners (1.5.2).

Context of Use describes the situation in which Users (1.1.2) perform *Work*. It includes any aspects of the *Work Context* exerting an influence on the worker, both physically or mentally. The descriptor is an aspect of the Approach (3.1.2.2). It relates to the Design Representation (2.1.1).

User Requirements describe the needs/wants/wishes/hopes of the User (1.1.2) as concerns any change in Human–Computer Technology (1.9), which they use. The descriptor relates to the Design Representation (2.1.1).

Design Solution (1.8.2) describes the result of solving a design problem. It relates to the Design Representation (2.1.1). It also relates to expressions of Performance (2.2.1).

6.2.2   Context of Use

'For context of use analysis, *Cognitive Work Analysis* is applied and in particular the *Contextual Activity Template*. The latter maps out all the system's functions and the different situations that end-users encounter. Also, *Tabular Task Analysis* is applied. The latter expresses the user's tasks in the subject-verb-object format. The format was used initially after seeing the sentence structure outlined in the book 'Guidelines for Developing Instructions' by Kay Inaba et al. (2004). It turned out to be a useful Approach (to *Task Analysis*. A template was created in Excel that divides up the elements of a user's tasks in this way. The Approach (3.1.2.2) allows development of *Task Analysis* in a consistent and systematic manner. At this stage, a record of an inventory of all the system's elements is created. For interactive systems, this involves recording each user interface screen and element. The Approach (3.1.2.2) accumulates large amounts of data, which have then to be reduced as needed.'

Guide Notes

Approach (3.1.2.2), as a descriptor, is superordinate to UX Practice (2.2.2).

Task Analysis reflects task activity and any associated behaviour. It is superordinate to *Cognitive Work Analysis*. It relates to Design Representation (2.1.1).

6.2.3   User Requirements

'To understand *User Requirements*, the relevant *Human Factors* parameters are applied to the context of use. Spreadsheets are compiled that contain *Principles, Patterns, Guidelines* etc. The source is recorded, a link to the source where applicable, and the key insights from the source. Also included are keywords for which to search. This allows filter and search for patterns across the data collected. It is a '*Commonplace*' Book. Any source of evidence is noted, if of help. Large numbers of *Principles*, *Patterns*, and *Guidelines* are applied. It is then a case of applying the right parameters to the situation.'

Guide Notes

Principles describe a type of design knowledge. *Principles* can be part of a Framework (3.1.2.1) or Approach (3.1.2.2). They contribute to Design Representations (2.1.1).

   Patterns describe common recurring elements of different Design Solutions (1.8.2) to the same Design Problem (1.8.2). Patterns can be part of a Framework (3.1.2.1) or Approach (3.1.2.2). *Patterns* contribute to Design Representations (2.1.1).

   Guidelines describe 'rules of thumb' or 'hints and tips' for good design. *Guidelines* can be part of a Framework (3.1.2.1) or Approach (3.1.2.2). They contribute to Design Representations (2.1.1).

6.2.4   Design Solutions

'Concerning the production of **Design Solutions** (1.8.2), a range of options is first identified. Then *Prototypes* for different possible solutions. For example, PowerPoint to simulate interactive user interfaces. The contribution favours how IDEO's CEO Brown talks about the need to 'build to think.' Also, the 'fail faster to succeed sooner' Approach (3.1.1.2).

   Design Solutions (1.8.1), assessed against the parameters identified earlier. For example, this might involve assessment against clauses from *Standards*, such as consistency of the positioning of controls. It might also involve **Performance** (3.3.1)-related parameters, such as task completion rates. Also collecting subjective, but quantifiable *Feedback* from users, acquired by means of the 'single ease question' and the '*system usability scale*'. Qualitative *Feedback* from Users (1.1.2) might also be collected.'

Guide Notes

Design Solution (1.8.1), as a descriptor, denotes the result of solving a Design Problem (1.8.1). It relates to Design Representation (2.1.1). It also relates to expressions of Performance (3.3.1).

   Approach (3.1.2.2) is present in the initial UX description. It is superordinate to UX Design Practice (2.3.2).

   Design Solution (1.8.1)—see earlier.

   Standards describe the prescriptions for effective design. They may be part of a Framework (3.1.2.1) or Approach (3.1.2.2). They contribute to Design Representations (2.1.1).

   Performance (3.3.1) expresses how well work is performed and at what resource cost to the user.

Identical Descriptors

Design Solutions (1.8.2)/Approach (3.1.1.2)/Performance (3.3.1).

Additional Descriptors

DesignPractice/ContextofUse/UserRequirements/TaskAnalysis/*Contextual-Activity Template*/CognitiveTaskAnalysis/TabularTaskAnalysis/Principles/Patterns/Guidelines/ Standards/Commonplace Book/Work/Work Context/Design Solutions.

Review

Grant's approach to framing design practice derives from UCD/HCI. As a result, it is contrastive with UX and light on associated references. However, there is a three descriptor overlap with the initial UX description. The sections comprise of Context of Use, User Requirements and Design Solutions. Two descriptors overlap with the initial UX description. The main relationship is subordination to more general descriptors. They can support a framework or approach. They contribute to design representations.

6.3   Cummaford Source Material (2022)

Summary

Cummaford's concept of 'best-practice' constitutes a de facto way of framing UX design practice. The necessary changes to current design practice to render it UX design practice are enumerated.

6.3.1   Framing UX Design Practice as Best-Practice (3.3.1)

'Revenue for *Digital Media* and technology in general, and e-commerce in particular, has grown. Turnover for e-commerce has increased from about £20 billion in 1998 to about £2 trillion per annum globally. [3] Hardly surprising then, that commercial *Best*-Practice (3.3.1) has attracted resources, resulting in its development and advancement. Future research needs to take account of how to apply current *Best*-Practice (3.3.1).
    Such changes in *Best*-Practice (3.3.1) follow:

1. From design for *Usability* to design for **User Experience** (1.3.2).
2. From design methods to Design *Methods* (3.1.2.3), enhanced by technical advances in *Data Capture.*
3. From simple online *Transaction Testing* to online *Design Funnel Testing.*
4. From simple online *Transaction Testing* to online *AB Testing.*
5. From *Structured Analysis and Design Methods* to 'Lean UX' *Design Methods.*
6. From the *Design Problem* to the *Minimum Viable Product'* (MVP).

7. From process design **Methods** (3.1.2.3) to '*Atomic*' *Design Methods*.
8. From individual online *User Testing* to online S*caled Up User Testing*.'

Guide Notes

Design for User Experience (1.2.2) (UX), as a descriptor, relates to framing UX design practice. Also, to UX Design Representation (2.3.1).

   Design Methods (3.1.2.3), as a descriptor, are enhanced by technical advances in *Data Capture*. They relate to UX Practice (2.2.2) and also, to UX Design Representation (2.3.1).

   Online Design Funnel Testing constitutes a form of UX Design Practice (3.3.2) and relates to UX Design Representation (2.1.2).

   Online AB Testing constitutes a form of UX Practice (2.2.2) and relates to UX Design Representation (2.1.2).

   Lean UX *Design Methods*, as a descriptor, constitute a form of UX Practice (2.2.2) and relate to UX Design Representation (2.1.2).

   Minimum Viable Product (*MVP*) relates to UX Practice (2.2.2) and also to UX Design Representation (2.1.2).

   Atomic Design Methods constitutes a form of UX Practice (2.2.2) and relates to UX Design Representation (2.1.2).

   Online Scaled Up User Testing constitutes a form of UX Practice (2.2.2) and relates to UX Design Representation (2.1.2).

Identical Features

Practice (3.3.1)/User Experience (1.3.2)/Methods (3.1.2.3).

Additional Features

Usability/Methods/Data Capture/Design for User Experience/Design/Data Capture/Design Methods/Online Funnel Testing/User Testing/Online AB Testing/Lean UX Design Methods/Minimal Viable Product/Atomic Design Methods/Online Scaled-Up User Testing/Digital Media.

Review

Cummaford's proposed changes to best-practice design to accommodate the requirements of UX, when taken together, constitute a way of framing UX design practice. Three descriptors overlap with those of the initial UX description, but many more relate at a lower level of description but not at the same level.

6.4   Chakraborty Source Material (2023)

Summary

Chakraborty's contribution proposes a novel framing for UX design practice, which takes the form of 'product-centric framing'. It includes the concepts of both framework and frame.

6.4.1   Product-Centric Framing

'**Framework** (3.1.2.1) and **Frame** (3.1.2.1), act as points of reference and an opportunity to simplify. They also perhaps help put in context the things that need to be thought about. Given that most things that get built are produced by companies, one useful way to re-frame is the *Product-Centric Framing*, which positions three intersecting circles, describing the cross-cutting concerns of *Business*, *Technology* and UX.' See Fig. 6.1 Product-Centric Framing.'

Guide Notes

Framework (3.1.2.1) and Frame (3.1.2.1), as descriptors, denote the structures, which support UX Practice (2.1.2). The descriptors can be expressed in a variety of ways. They are in contrast to, and more formed than, Approaches (3.1.2.2).

  Product-Centric Framing describes the intersection of *Business*, *Technology* and UX. The contrast is with user/customer-centric framing, human–computer interaction-centric framing and experience-centred design framing (ECD). [2] The descriptor is part of UX Practice (2.1.2). Products are designed, manufactured, marketed and sold.

Fig. 6.1 Product-centric framing

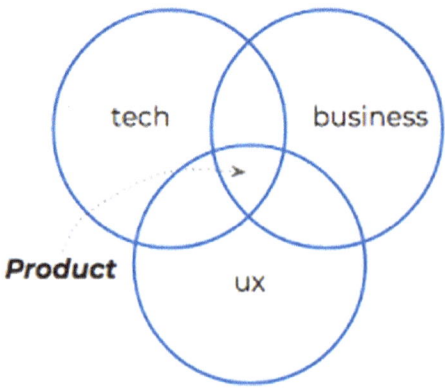

Business involves the designing, manufacturing, marketing and selling of products. The latter include those related to construction, health, education and commerce. The descriptor is an aspect of UX Practice (2.1.2).

Technology describes the application of scientific and engineering knowledge to the practical aims of human life. Also, to the change and transformation of the human environment. Types of *Technology* include mechanical, medical and communication. They contrast with culture or nature. The descriptor helps to frame UX Practice (2.1.2).

Identical Descriptors

Framework (3.1.1.1)/Frame (3.1.1.1).

Additional Descriptors

Product-Centric Framing/Business/Technology.

Review

Chakraborty proposes a novel framing for UX design practice—'product-centric framing'. It includes the concepts of both frames and frameworks for UX. The overlap is with two initial UX descriptors. For further details, other than relating to framing UX design practice, see 8.2. There are many initial UX descriptor superordinate relations.

6.5   Blyth Source Material (2023)

Summary

Blyth presents a completely novel way of framing UX design practice. It takes the form of personal muses. Six such muses are identified and described. Their sections comprise—Art and Delight, Pragmatism and Shipping, Persuasion, Dark Patterns, Tech-First Innovation and AI Design. The novel concept of 'experience quality' is also proposed.

6.5.1   Introduction

'Here, I will consider a number of these inspirations—*Muses*, if you will—as a way to define and challenge 'what UX is'. As the journey unfolds, we will start to consider UX as a subset in the wider notion of *Quality*.

The *Muses* I present here are personal, any journeyman reader will have their own. Each one has, since the turn of the century, presented the possibility that UX **Practice** (3.3.1) is neither necessary nor sufficient for *Quality* to exist. And yet, crucially, the further we travel from UX, from its modes and focus (and those of *Usability* before it) the more important a *Homecoming* feels.'

Guide Notes

Muse, as a descriptor, is traditionally considered to be a source of artistic inspiration. Here, the *Muses* are those personal to Blyth as a UX Practitioner (1.5.2).

UX denotes User Experience (1.3.2), both as undergone by the User (1.1.2) and designed for by the Practitioner (1.5.2).

Practice denotes UX design activity, as in Specification (1.8.2).

Quality characterises the nature of Experience (1.3.2).

Usability describes a criterion of Performance (2.2.1), typically expressed in terms of the speed and errors of task Performance (2.2.1).

Homecoming denotes the return from an Odyssey. The contrast is with 'leaving' or 'departing'.

6.5.2   Muse 1: The Muse of Art and Delight

'In 2014, at the UXPA International Conference, I presented my thoughts on my recent experiences designing with and for Artists and *Performers* (https://amt-lab.org/blog/2021/10/artistic-futures-digital-interactive-installations). In this domain, the usual precepts of UX thinking are hard to follow. I described two particular cases.

First, the **User** (1.1.2) is staged as an artistic performer. In this case, a layman User (1.1.2) is engaged with a '*Walk up and Use*' *interface* that has an artistic intention. Consider the great many *Interactive Installations* that are now found at so many festivals, civic events and corporate head office entrance foyers. (https://amt-lab.org/blog/2021/10/artistic-futures-digital-interactive-installations).

Second, an *Artistic Performer* is cast as a *Use (1.1.2)*. Examples such as the interactive gloves of musician Imogen Heap (https://www.youtube.com/watch?v=ci-yB6EgVW4) or the completely bespoke musical instruments of Kraftwek or Harry Partch (https://www.bbc.co.uk/music/articles/b49cbf91-9172-4881-9501-7fb5f87700a5).

Many of these interfaces are designed exclusively for the use of one single performer. The design and the **Performance** (3.3.1) become almost indistinguishable.

In 2014, I continued to argue that the motivations of art and self-expression were difficult, if not impossible, to reconcile with the motivations of **User Experience** (1.3.2), as it is usually understood.

In the first case, the end goal of the interaction is an artistic expression. The creation of spectacle, or mystery, may be part of that. These multi-sensory immersive experiences are often geared for gentle sensory outcomes, or surprising moments of delight. All of these outcomes are not usually thought to be in the dominion of UX.

In the second case, the performer and their sense of performance identity and agency needs to be in harmony with the creation of a completely novel tool. It is very difficult to imagine this individualistic quality arising from the typical methods in the UX toolkit.

To be clear, in the last twenty years many UX theorists have included conceptions of delight, or emotion, or affect, in their models of UX. In fact this was one of the key notions that distinguished UX from traditional 'system usability'. But it is hard to imagine that there is any practical way to operationalise these ideas so that they will be of utility to artists and performers working with the kinds of interactive systems described above. Yet, designed and built they are, and undeniable in terms of *Quality*, in the eyes of the right audience, in the right context.'

Guide Notes

Interactive Installation, as a descriptor, is subordinate to Human–Computer Technology (1.3.2) and superordinate to website. Such installations are to be found at festivals and civic events, among others.

Performance (3.3.1) denotes how well a task is performed, typically in terms of speed and errors.

Delight/Emotion/Affect are all Experiences (1.2.2), for which UX attempts to design.

System Usability describes a criterion of interactive Performance (3.3.1), in terms of how easy it is for a User (1.1.2) to perform a task.

Quality is a new concept, which denotes the degree of excellence of Experience (1.2.2), undergone or encountered by a User (1.1.2).

6.5.3   Muse 2: The Muse of Pragmatism and Shipping

'UX *Careers* tend to follow one of a number of templates. It may be from 'junior' to 'senior' or 'individual contributor' to 'manager'. Another common path for UX **Practitioners** (1.5.2), in the last twenty years, has been to move from UX *Research* to UX *Design* and then into *Product Management*. This progression is mirrored in many other professions: from understanding, to creating, to governing. From the many UX (1.5.2) that have followed this path, there is a common reflection: 'I only know now how easy it is to criticise something, but how hard it is to solve it'. (https://rosenfeldmedia.com/books/product-management-for-ux-people/).

UX Practitioners (1.5.2) are well known to be harsh critics. Indeed, it is part of the core of their role in many organisations, be it through *Expert Reviews*, or *Design Critiques*, or primary-research based UX *Evaluations*. An experienced UX Practitioner (1.5.2) will deconstruct an experience or an interface and present winning solutions that will engender greater satisfaction and deeper, more successful user interactions. That is what they are there to do.

As UXers obtain more experience and become more familiar with the implications of these winning solutions, for example development costs, or opportunity costs, they will of course start to see the bigger picture to what was previously 'a no brainer for better User Experience' (1.3.2). This is a crucial part of the maturity of a Practitioner (1.5.2), and the ability to converse in these terms separates out the juniors from the seniors. This is what leads in the world of UX.

One of the most impactful ways, many UX Practitioners (1.5.2) will get this perspective, is to act in the role of a *Product Manager*. What might be obvious as the best design for User Experience (1.3.2), as one aspect of the product, suddenly becomes low priority, when faced with the harsh reality that doing this work means that Users (1.1.2) will not get other work done elsewhere. This balancing of UX impact versus effort is the touchstone of a *Product Manager's* role. Further to that, they must also address the equally important ambitions of a never-ending list of other non-UX focused initiatives. *Quality*, for a *Product Manager*, has UX at its heart, but it cannot be in thrall to the concept.

Pragmatic decisions take over, and the primary concern often becomes one of '*Shipping*'. A system focused on perfect User Experience may be something to which to aspire. But if it is unreleased, it will never beat the lesser system that nonetheless actually gets into *User's* hands.

The challenge to UX here is to recognise that it is really only one part of the puzzle of the creation of *Quality*.'

Guide Notes

UX Practitioner (1.5.2), as a descriptor, denotes someone who designs for User Experience (1.3.2).

Product Management describes the planning and control of products and the people performing these functions. The contrast is with product design and product manufacture.

Expert Reviews/Design Critiques/UX Evaluation are types of UX *Assessment*. They contrast with *Design*, but are part of UX Practice (2.2.2).

Shipping denotes the release of a product, for example, an application.

User Experience (1.3.2) denotes experience undergone by the User (1.1.2) and designed for by the UX Practitioner (1.5.2).

Users denote people using *Interactive Systems* with intent to do something, as desired.

Product Management/User Experience/—see earlier.

6.5.4   Muses 3 and 4: The Muses of Persuasion and Dark Patterns

'Another stepping stone on the path from *Usability* to UX, and beyond, was the attempt to harness psychological and cognitive understanding to make products not just emotional, or affective, but also in some way behaviour changing. The foremost proponent of this concept has been Fogg at the Stanford Persuasive Technology Lab (https://www.amazon.co.uk/Peruasive-Technology-Computers-Interactive-/Technologies/dp/1558606432)'. A variety of interactive design techniques have been researched and documented by Fogg. These include compelling trigger/notification sound design, to full gamification of apps and other day-to-day systems.

This concept has been another provocation for those in UX. Is their role to act entirely for the benefit of their *User Stakeholders*? Should tools empower Users or change Users (1.1.2)? Fogg has taken great pains to specify the parameters of *Ethical Persuasion*. But this stance was not embraced by Eyal, whose bestselling 2014 book 'Hooked: How To Build Habit Forming Products' feels scarcely palatable after the subsequent decade of mass *Social Media* manipulation that has been so well documented.

Rowing back from unethical behaviour manipulation, and into more familiar 'true UX' waters, we might find ourselves with Brignull and his colleagues who have spent many years documenting *Deceptive Design* (aka *Dark Patterns*, https://www.deceptive.design/). This inversion of the practices of the behaviour manipulation experts identifies corporates and others who practise these tricks and publicly names and shames them. The team also works in legal contexts to advise on and help enforce laws that are intended to prevent manipulative interactive design.

Any UX Practitioner (1.5.2) being drawn into these themes in the last twenty years must surely also conclude that a principal part of UX, of the *Quality* of its offer, is its 'pro bono publico' nature.

NB: A decade after publishing 'Hooked', and trading on its advice, it would seem that Eyal reached the same conclusions, by authoring a new volume by the name of 'Indistractibe: How To Control Your Attention'. One might regard this new work as some kind of atonement. Or, alternatively, an escalation in his own personal arms race with himself.'

Guide Notes

Usability, as a descriptor, denotes a criterion of interactive system Performance (2.2.1).

UX denotes User Experience (1.3.2), both as undergone by the User (1.1.2) and designed for by the Practitioner (1.5.2).

User Stakeholders denote other people affected by designs, which target the end User (1.1), for example, the latter's management. The time a User (1.1.2) spends working may be reduced by distractions, such as viewing unrequested advertisements.

Ethical Persuasion implies some form of *Moral Acceptability*. The contrast is with *Deceptive Design*.

Deceptive Design/Dark Patterns describe manipulative and possibly unethical UX Practice (2.3.2). The contrast is with empowering a User's (1.1.2) behaviour.

UX Practitioner (1.5.2) denotes someone directly involved in designing the interfaces for interactive systems.

Quality characterises the degree of excellence of Experience (1.3.2), undergone or encountered by a User (1.1.2).

6.5.5   Muse 5: The Muse of Tech-first Innovation

'Among UX *Practitioners*, it is an article of faith the User (1.1.2) is the centre of the *Design Process*. Some Practitioners (1.5.2) insist that they are foremost psychologists, and that they can design for any technology because the human condition does not change. They warn against the very worst crime of all, that solutions should ever be dictated by technology, rather than by a pure understanding of *User Need*.

All this is true, to a point. For the Class of 2000, it was easy to confidently smash the looms of the technophiles and neophytes who bullishly insisted on new features based on barely usable early technologies. Clunky touchscreen devices, awkward VR headsets, stuttering video meeting technology, abysmal speech synthesis and recognition, irrelevant QR codes. These and a hundred other 'all tech, no *Use Case*' ideas were battlegrounds for 'tech-first' versus 'user-first' advocates.

But while these battles were underway, and the UX *Community* were proud of their wins in the name of their Users (1.1.2), others were quietly creating early applications of these technologies, building early adopter User (1.1.2) bases, refining products and, ultimately, contributing to the development of the actual technologies until everyone finally gained adoption, and many became themselves mainstays of 'good' User Experience (1.3.2).

The challenge posed to UX here is—can it be allowed for designs to be built and promoted that are clearly too early to be successful, as some kind of selfless act of allowing nascent technologies to flourish?'

Guide Notes

UX Practitioner (1.5.2), as a descriptor, denotes someone directly involved in designing the interfaces for interactive systems.

User (1.1.2) denotes people using *Interactive Systems* with intent to do something, as desired.

UX denotes User Experience (1.3.2), both as undergone by the User (1.1.2) and designed for by the Practitioner (1.5.2).

Users (1.1.2) denote people using *Interactive Systems* with intent to do something, as desired.

User Need equates to user requirement, more generally.

Use Case is part of the *Design Process*, based on user requirements. The contrast is with technical requirements.

UX/*Users*—see earlier.

User Experience (1.3.2) denotes experience undergone by the User (1.1.2) and designed for by the UX *Practitioner*.

6.5.6   Muse 6: The Muse of AI Design

'2022 and 2023 have seen a breathtaking acceleration of the public understanding of, and appetite for, *Artificial Intelligence* products. The headline-grabbing *AI* darling *Chat GPT* proved to be the fastest growing consumer product in history, reaching 100 million active monthly users in just two months (https://www.reuters.com/technology/chatgpt-sets-record-fastest-growing-user-base-analyst-note-2023-02-01/). Dall-e and Midjourney were following suit with barely believable monthly advances in artistic novel image generation.

If anyone assumed that the revolution would imperil only the jobs of low skilled workforce, they were quickly disabused of this notion. Creative *Illustrators* and *Copywriters* suddenly found themselves under existential threat.

Is UX Practice (2.2.2) next? For sure, in early 2023, with a little guidance the tools can write the copy and create convincing visual mockups. But that is far from true UX thinking and practice. For *AI* to generate successful products and experiences, it would need to be trained on the datasets of similar successful experiences.

Quickly, the muse of *AI* Design looks more like a siren. By participating in the undeniably diverting promise of *AI*, Practitioners (1.5.2) are training the very systems that will potentially soon relieve them of their responsibilities. Like those illustrators and content creators before them, we see UX designers today sleepwalking into the kind of practice that once had Oppenheimer reaching for his copy of the Bhagavad-Gita.

In any case, this particular revolution began some time ago with the availability of *Big Data* in online systems.

For many years already, our User Experiences (1.3.2) have included many dynamically composed lists. Think of a TV set with refreshing lists of popular channels, a website with algorithmically generated recommended books or products, a *Worksystem* with dynamically created 'next best actions' and so on. It has been the case for some time that a designer of any system really cannot know what a particular user is seeing on their screen without having a profile of that user.

However, this is changing with the advent of generative user experiences. To be clear, these are not Experiences (1.3.2) that are created by designers with *AI* tools, researching with samples of six participants, or *Usage Data* from six million.

These are experiences (1.3.2) that are themselves created by generative *AI* systems (https://prototypr.io/post/generative-ai-design). The servers will optimise not just individual dynamic components, but entire *Workflows* to achieve optimal results. The system will measure success of outcomes and modify Experiences (1.3.2) accordingly, for every user. The complexity of a *User Profile*, and the amount of flexibility within a *Generative Interface* will be so profound (and, of course, in a *Machine Learning Blackbox*), that it will be impossible for a human Practitioner (1.5.2) to know or even predict what Experience (1.3.2) any one user is having. And so what role for UX in this new world? What does *Quality* look like when you don't get to see it?

We know that *AI* systems can only generate alternatives, if they are given parameters to measure success against. What are the metrics of success that could be used? A range of output metrics, such as *Engagement* and *Profit*, no doubt. But also we are surely drawn back to three well-researched and well known measures of a system, familiar now for more than twenty years. Namely: *Effectiveness, Efficiency and Satisfaction*.

Could it be so simple?'

Guide Notes

Artificial Intelligence/AI, as a descriptor, denotes software, that aims to exhibit human-like intelligence, with which it contrasts.

Quality characterises a wider state of Experience (1.3.2)—its degree of excellence.

6.5.7   After the Muses, a *Homecoming*

'At the start of this piece I explained that I would outline an *Odyssey* that would be familiar to many UX Practitioners (1.5.2) in the last twenty years. The *Muses* I have identified are definitely personal, but also shared by many individuals, and by the UX *Community* itself.'

And so what becomes of a practitioner undertaking this journey? What impact of the *Muses*? Each one alone is enough to inspire a completely different destination. Those paths are engaging, intellectually satisfying, and likely well remunerated.

For many UX *Practitioners*, the position is one that is adopted intimately, and will perhaps forever colour their perceptions. Even as we dalliance with alternative paths and *Muses* such as the ones described here, UX is never far from mind, and it influences even the most unlikely of projects and topics. Like Popper's scientific method, UX *Practice* is 'a way of operating' that will likely never depart, and will always be of use.

To stand at one remove from our own experiences, we might also think about the qualities of a new practitioner that we would want to join our team, if we were trying to create a *Quality User Experience* for an as-yet-unknown context. Would it be advisable to choose the person dipping their toes into art and **Performance** (3.3.1)? Or a product manager in the making? A behaviour change advocate or protector? A tech enthusiast? An AI entrepreneur? No, we would be advised to choose someone with very traditional UX skills. Someone that can understand real *User Needs* and engineer solutions to truly satisfy them.

But then: If a pure UX mindset is of such great value, to what end are these *Muses* of any benefit to anyone? If a *Homecoming* is proper and desirable, what is the point of it all? Well, we might think of these professional and intellectual *Muses* as grist to the mill. While each one would be a legitimate pursuit on its own terms, perhaps their true value lies in the journey itself, the lessons therein, and their compound interaction with each other and with the original core set of *HCI* and UX values. Learning from one amplifies the skills learned in the other. They afford unexpected evolution to us—as practitioners, yes—but also as agents in the world. As people.

And what was supposedly 'work' all along was in fact growth. Here, in the final analysis, I am reminded of Pirsig writing in 1974: "The real cycle you're working on is a cycle called yourself."

Guide Notes

Odyssey, as a descriptor, denotes a long journey full of adventures. Also, a series of experiences that give knowledge or understanding to someone. Both appear to be implicated here.

UX Practitioners (1.5.2) denote designers of human-interaction Experiences (1.3.2).

Muse is traditionally considered to be a source of artistic inspiration. Here, the *Muses* are personal to Blyth.

UX *Community* might equate to UX Movement (1.4.2) or UX field of study, as a general description.

UX denotes User Experience (1.3.2), both as undergone by the User (1.1.2) and designed for by the UX Practitioner (1.5.2).

Muse/UX Practitioners/UX—see earlier.

Quality User Experience is a novel concept, which extends the meaning of User Experience (1.3.2) to include its degree of excellence.

Homecoming is an instance of returning home, in this case from an *Odyssey*.

HCI denotes humans interacting with computers as desired and intended.

Identical Descriptors

User (1.1.2)/Performance (3.3.1)/Practitioner (1.5.2)/User Experience (1.3.2)/Practice (2.2.1).

Additional Descriptors

Muse/UX/Practice/Quality/Usability/Homecoming/Interactive   Installation/Delight Emotion   Affect/System   Usability/Quality/UX   Practitioners/ProductManagement/ ExpertReview/DesignCritique/UXEvaluation/Shipping/User experience/Users/Big Data/ Worksystem/Blackbox/Machine   Learning/Generative   Interface/Engagement/Profit/ Illustrators/Copywriters/Usage Data/Workflows/AI/Artificial Intelligence/User Stakeholders/Ethical Persuasion/Deceptive Design/Dark Patterns/User Need/Use case/Artificial Intelligence/AI/Odyssey/UX Community/HCI/Efficiency/Effectiveness/Satisfaction.

Review

Blyth presents a new way of framing UX and so a new way of framing UX design practice. It takes the form of personal Muses. These include art and delight, pragmatism and shipping, persuasion and dark patterns, tech-first innovation and AI design. There is a very inclusive five descriptor overlap with the initial UX description. Subordinate descriptor relations, however, also abound.

Chapter Review

The practitioner source material contributions are presented, as they describe framing UX design practice. The initial UX description is applied to the source material, as part of the process of constructing a final description. Although all the contributions address framing UX design practice, they do so in very different ways. Grant's approach derives from UCD/HCI. As a result, it is contrastive with UX and light on associated references. Cummaford's concept of 'best-practice' constitutes a de facto way of framing UX design practice. The necessary changes to current design practice to render it UX design practice are enumerated. Chakraborty's contribution proposes a novel framing for UX design practice, which takes the form of 'product-centric' framing. It includes the concepts of both framework and frame. Last, Blyth presents a completely novel way of framing UX design practice. It takes the form of personal muses. Six such muses are identified and described.

The overlap with the initial UX description is varies from modest to inclusive. Many additional descriptors are, however, identified. The latter relate primarily as subordinate to descriptors in the UX description.

Chapter Carry Forward

The carry-forward from Chaps. 4–10 appears in Appendix 1. It constitutes the basis for the initial UX description and hence for the guide to framing design practice for UX. The appendix is intended to support readers in applying the initial UX description to the UX practitioner source material. Also, in completing the associated exercise assignments, Appendix 1 is not for reading as a text in itself, but for consultation in its application.

6.6   Exercise Assignment

The exercise assignment is intended to test readers' understanding and application of the concepts presented. Also to support their tailoring the initial UX description to their own design requirements.

Consulting 6.2 to 6.5

– *Check* the shared descriptors between the initial UX description and the UX source material.
– *Do you agree* with the descriptors identified? If not, then
– *Compile* your own list.

– *Justify* your listing.

– *Add* to the descriptor identification listing any changes, implied in or additional to, your completion of the Exercise Assignment 3.8.
– *How* do your changes add to the completeness, coherence and fitness-for-purpose of the descriptors? Justify your claims.

Select a UX paper of your own, of a colleague or of your supervisor.

Consulting 6.2 to 6.5.

– *Identify* in *Italics* additional descriptors appearing in the paper.
– *Identify* in **Bold** descriptors identical to those of the initial UX description.
– *Compare* the identical and additional descriptors identified with those identified here.
– *Note* the similarities.
– *Note* the differences.
– *Compare* similarities and the differences.
– *Assess* the comparison.
– *Reflect* and *Conclude* on the comparison.
– *Give* your reasons.

6.7   Notes

[1] Although the 'centre' highlighted by each of these approaches differs, this does not exclude other descriptors/factors being in common. For example, 'user' in both product-centric and human-centric design.
[2] These figures date from 2022.

Reference

Inaba, K., Parsons, S.O., Smillie, R.M. (2004). https://api.taylorfrancis.com.

UX Practitioner Source Material Describing UX Frameworks

7

7.1 Introduction

The chapter presents source material for framing design practice for UX. They take the form of frameworks. The same guide summary/review structure of 4.1 is used here. Likewise for the concepts and their relations. To crosscheck the UX contributions with the initial UX descriptors, see Appendix 1.

7.2 Chakraborty Source Material (2023)

Summary

Chakraborty proposes a novel framing for UX design practice. It takes the form of a 'product-centric' frame. It equates to a UX framework. Only a high-level description at this time, its potential as a framework, however, is self-evident.

7.2.1 Product-Centric Framework

'The *Topic* of UX is complex and struggles with *Definition*, *Scope*, and *Perceived Utility*. At the same time, everyone wants it, feels it's important and yet no-one completely owns it. *Experience* is unique; mine is mine and yours is yours and yet design would get quite complicated without some commonality, a set of norms, rules of thumb or good old-fashioned principles'.

The UX **Approaches** (3.1.2.2), of the late 90s, early 2000s, were largely based on a *Linear Development Cycle*, where ideas are conceived, *Requirements* are gathered, *Designs*

Fig. 7.1 Product-centric
framework

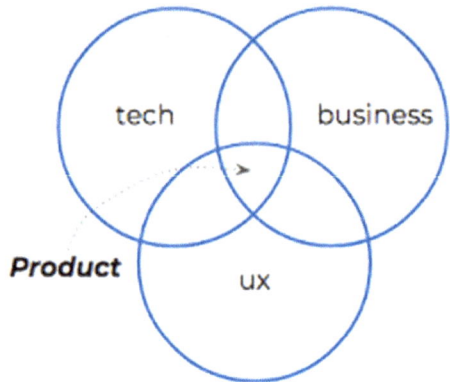

are built, tests are conducted and eventually the 'thing' is launched and needs to be operated and maintained.

Since the start of the 2000s, consider how the *Growth in Technology* has become exponential and reshaped every aspect of our lives. From *Mobility* to *Metaverse*, *Internet of Things* to *Augmented Reality*, the world of *Experience* has become rather too complicated and while UX has become essential, it inhabits an uncomfortable space, where it's tricky to define and problematic to own. The UX designer's role (assuming there is such a role in a company) and so their work is often confined to designing a few *Widgets* for the webpage.

Frameworks (3.1.2.1) and **Frames** (3.1.2.1), act as points of reference and an opportunity to simplify. They also perhaps help put in context the things that need to be thought about. Given that most things that get built are produced by companies, one useful way to re-frame is the *Product-Centric Framing*, which positions three intersecting circles, describing the cross-cutting concerns of *Business*, *Technology* and UX. The *Product-Centric Framework* is shown in Fig. 7.1.

Consider the choice of a microprocessor, sitting in the intersection. The technology consideration is relatively clear, encompassing requirements to do with chip fabrication, semi-conductor quality and number of transistors. The business consideration will be largely to do with the bill of materials. Choices may be impacted by inflationary pressures, impacts on supply chain and any other political dimension, for instance, China's blockade of ships to Taiwan. The UX angle will be that the chip will need to both be compatible with the operating systems, the applications and that they perform at the right speed to deliver the right experience.

At this level of framing, it's straightforward to appreciate that *Functional* and *Nonfunctional* requirements that need to be satisfied in the building of a 'thing'. The trillions of things in existence today, whether they be physical hardware devices, component parts of devices, websites, smartphone screens, in car displays, 3D headsets, the UX challenge becomes staggeringly complex.

Guide Notes

Topic, as a descriptor, has the same or similar meaning to possible superordinates, such as 'field' or Movement (1.4.2). Its meaning, however, is very general. More like the 'whole idea of' or even just the 'subject matter of'. Alternatively, *Topic* might identify a UX field of study or a *UX Community*. It is an acceptable alternative to Movement (1.4.2).

UX denotes User Experience (1.3.2) as encountered or undergone or as designed for.

Definition is assumed to be required for UX. The 'struggle' derives from different views on its nature and content. Also to the vagueness absence of such views altogether.

Scope defines the UX descriptor Particular Scope (1.8.2). The latter relates to the UX General Problem of Design (1.7.2).

Perceived Utility relates to UX Performance (2.2.1). It is a criterion of interactive system Performance (2.2.1). It is also superordinate to Human–Computer Technology (1.10). A more formed expression of UX would require the scoping of its concepts, including *Topic, Definition and Perceived Utility*.

Experience denotes individual Conscious Events (1.3.2), which are unique. However, they can still be designed for. Also, as one of the shared ideas the UX Movement (1.4.2) is working to advance. Users (1.1.2) may have the same intent, at some level of description, for example paying a bill by Internet banking. But the individual experience of realising that specific intent is unique.

Linear Development Cycle denotes a form of superordinate serial design. The *Cycle* is no longer espoused by UX Practitioners (1.5.2). It has been replaced by less serial forms.

Growth in Technology is superordinate to *Mobility, Metaverse, Internet of Things* and *Augmented Reality*.

Internet is populated by *Websites*, which buy and sell products and services and also provide general information. The contrast is with offline sources, such as high-street shops.

Product-Centric Framing denotes a novel UX Framework (3.1.2.1).

Business includes marketing, financing, logistics and so on. The descriptor impacts UX Practice (2.2.2) and UX Performance (2.2.2).

Technology is superordinate to Human–Computer Technology (1.10).

7.2.2   UX Key Ideas

(1) 'UX is dead, long live UX
(2) How does a *Product-Centric Frame* for UX help?
(3) How do you do UX at speed in the *Era of Exponential*?'

Guide Notes

UX is strikingly juxtaposed as both dead and alive. The description underlines the disagreements within the UX Movement (1.4.2). Also, the difficulties of specifying its *Definition*, *Scope* and *Perceived Utility*.

Product-Centric is a novel descriptor, as well as a UX Framework (3.1.2.1). It links to business, markets, management and also to *Perceived Utility*. It contrasts with user-centric, consumer-centric and experience-centric.

Era of Exponential refers to the rate at which new digital technology is developed, the speed of its market penetration and the range of its applications.

Identical Descriptors

UX Approaches (3.1.2.2)/Framework (3.1.1.1))/Frame (3.1.1.1).

Additional Descriptors

Topic/Definition/Scope/Perceived Utility/Experience/Linear Development Cycle/Growth of Technology/Internet of Things/Mobility/Metaverse/Augmented Reality/Product-Centric Framing/Functional/Non-functional/Business/Technology/Widgets/Product-Centric/Era of Exponential.

Review

Chakraborty characterises UX frameworks in terms of frame and framing. He proposes a novel 'product-centric' framework with which to frame UX design practice. Its key ideas are presented. Three descriptors overlap the initial UX description. Subordinate descriptors, however, are also presented.

7.3   Timmer Source Material (2010)

Summary

Timmer proposes a novel framing for UX design practice. It takes the form of a UX design for performance framework. The structure is explicit and detailed. The relations between elements are identified. Text provides additional clarification. The framework sections comprises of the following Dowell and Long's Conception, Performance, Desired/Actual Performance and Diagnosis/Prescription.

7.3.1   Design for Performance Framework for UX

The general description of the framework is that of performance for UX.

7.3.2   Dowell and Long's Conception

'The contribution begins by citing parts of Dowell and Long's (1989) *Conception* of the *Cognitive Engineering* Design Problem. *Conception* here equates to **Framework** (3.1.2.1) and is used from now on. However, it is not alone, in its attempt to outline the fundamental components of an engineering discipline of '*Cognitive Design*'. It has, however, been chosen, less because of its emphasis on '*Cognitive Behaviour*' leading the *Design Process*. But more on deficiency of '**Performance**' (3.3.1), followed by respecification of the *Worksystem*. The latter including importantly a human '*Cognitive*' Component.

The latter supports the creation of Business 'Customers', as a means of addressing a *Design Solution* to the *Design Problem*. The user's cognition drives their action, thereby progressing them through the *Conversion Funnel*. A button may be rendered larger, and brighter, to capture a customer's mental process of '*Attention*' (Long and Baddeley, 1984). A clear table may support better 'Reasoning' about a choice (Buckley and Long, 1990). The reasoning might support the desired user 'click' behaviour. The latter to improve *Performance Data* towards businesses desired performance levels. Hence, aligning *Design Problem* with *Design Solution*.'

Guide Notes

Conception, as a descriptor, is a structure for supporting thinking and reasoning about something. It equates with Framework (3.1.2.1).

Design Problem denotes the difference between actual and desired performance.

Design Solution denotes actual and desired performance being the same.

7.3.3   Performance

By attributing a measurement of quality and cost to an expression of Performance (3.3.1), cognitive engineers have somewhere to start the diagnosis process. Also, application of the concepts of '*Desired*' and '*Actual*' levels of Performance (3.3.1) assist in the framing of a Design Problem. First, the business needs to be able to express *Desired Performance*. This is likely to be in aggregate terms and largely referencing *Task Quality*. The latter, in terms of the number of occasions the *Worksystem* generated 'valid and fulfillable' orders. Also, the total value of those orders, against some measurement of *Cost* (expense).

The latter in supporting the *Digital Channel* to the consumer. Performance (3.3.1) is also likely to make reference to the missed opportunity in terms of low *Task Quality* and high *User Costs*. In addition, orders abandoned in the *Conversion Funnel* ('work' left undone in the domain), time to progress through the *Conversion Funnel* at each step, complaints and customer satisfaction ratings (*Worksystem* costs). It is by measuring *Actual*

Performance in terms of such criteria that *Web Site Analytics*, (and wider *Business Intelligence*), provide the cognitive engineer with a valuable toolset. The latter supporting Performance (3.3.1) measurement and *Design Problem Diagnosis*.'

Guide Notes

Task Quality, as a descriptor, denotes how well a task is performed. Along with *User Costs*, it expresses Performance (3.3.1).

User Costs describe the resource costs (mental and physical) to the User (1.1.2) performing the task as well as they do.

Desired Performance is in contrast to *Actual Performance*. The former is the target Performance (3.3.1), which the designer is trying to achieve with a new design. The latter is the Performance (3.3.1) achieved with the current version. If *Desired Performance* equals *Actual Performance*, there is no *Design Problem*. If, however, *Desired Performance* is different from (usually more than) *Actual Performance*, there is a *Design Problem*.

Actual Performance is in contrast to *Desired Performance*. The former describes current performance, which the designer is trying to change (usually to improve), as concerns the present design. The latter is the target Performance (3.3.1) for the new version. If *Actual Performance* equals *Desired Performance*, there is no *Design Problem*. If, however, *Actual Performance* is different from (usually less than) *Desired Performance*, there is a *Design Problem*.

7.3.4   Desired Performance

'The engineering **Approach** (3.1.2.2) for UX relies on the business to express *Desired Performance*. Once this is expressed, however, means are required for measuring the *Actual Performance*. By tagging pages across the site; modelling *User Journeys* and paths therethrough; measuring the time spent on each page; comparing this to the value of the basket at each step, only then can measurements of *Actual Performance* (of individual prospective customers) can be aggregated into summary statistics. The latter are models of Performance (3.3.1) that support diagnosis. That is, diagnosis of points in the *Customer Journey*, where Performance (3.3.1) begins to deteriorate in terms of *Desired Performance*. Diagnosis may start from pages, where Performance (3.3.1) deteriorates beyond repair. Also, instances where prospective customers are lost from the funnel (and wider site) completely. They are 'bounced' away. Further, from pages where time spent before advancement appears unusually long, as hesitancy and uncertainty sets in. *Web-Site Analytics* provide granular and aggregated data to support the cognitive engineer in *Diagnosis*. Also, Reasoning about why the *Performance Data* are as measured. And so further about the origins of a plausible *Design Problem*. The latter being the one under consideration.'

Guide Notes

User Journey denotes the website navigation, required to attain the user goals. It is one of, and perhaps the most common UX descriptor. It appears in the vast majority of source contributions. It is subordinate to the UX Design Representation.

Customer Journey denotes the website navigation, required to attain the customer goals. See also the preceding *User Journey*. It is subordinate to the UX Design Representation (3.2.1).

7.3.5   Diagnosis and Prescriptions

'Scientific (or other) hypotheses are part of a scientific (or other) method to generate scientific (or other) knowledge that supports better 'explanation' (or other) and prediction (or other) processes [1]. In contrast, cognitive engineering [2] develops a set of *Diagnoses*. When these are addressed during the cognitive engineering process of *Prescription* (specification), it improves and aligns the worksystem's Performance (3.3.1) data. The better to match the businesses desired level of Performance (3.3.1). If uplift is not possible, the digital channel may disappear as a candidate *User Experience* choice for prospective customers, when interacting with the business.

Diagnosis then needs to go beyond an Approach (3.1.2.2) of applied science (or other). Instead it needs to consider the *User Journey* to a point where Performance (3.3.1) deteriorates. In addition to the page, where deterioration is most marked. Hypotheses need to be generated by the cognitive engineer that draw upon all the disciplines that support cognitive design (attention, reasoning, vision), to explain the Performance (3.3.1) design problem. The abandonment of a basket at the page before confirmation may have little to do with a problem with the order summary page itself. Quite the opposite is possible, if the *User Journey* is examined. The order summary page may reveal the true transportation expense of the 'valid and fulfillable' order, expenses. Were the latter known earlier, this would have resulted in fewer prospective customers abandoning their order at such a late stage. *Diagnoses* need to consider the *Customer Journey*, and the mental events that the pages support, such as '*True Order Cost Realisation*'. *Prescriptions* then follow, in the form of *Design Specifications* that address the *Diagnosis*. The claim that the *Design Problem* is thus solved constitutes and concludes the contribution.'

Guide Notes

Diagnosis identifies a *Design Problem*. The contrast is with *Prescription*, which identifies a *Design Solution*. They both derive from the Framework (3.1.2.1) for UX.

Prescription identifies a *Design Solution*. The contrast is with *Diagnosis*, which identifies a *Design Problem*. They both derive from the Framework (3.1.2.1) for UX.

Identical Descriptors

Performance (3.3.1)/Framework (3.1.2.1)/Approach (3.1.2.2).

Additional Descriptors

Conception/Design Problem/Design Solution/Task Quality/User Costs/Desired Performance/Cognitive Engineering/Digital Channel/Business Intelligence/Design Process/Conversion Funnel/Attention/Cognitive Design/Cognitive Behaviour/Actual Performance/User Journey/Performance Data/Customer Journey/Worksystem/Cognitive Component/Diagnosis/Prescription.

Review

Timmer's contribution to framing UX design practice is a UX design for performance framework. The latter comprises sections on Desired/Actual Performance and Diagnosis/Prescription. There is a three descriptor identical overlap with the initial UX description. There is also overlap of a relational kind both of subordination and of superordination.

7.4   Middlemass Source Material (2023)

Summary

Middlemass proposes a novel framing for UX design practice—the XD playbook framework. The structure is explicit and detailed. The relations between elements are identified. Notes provide additional clarification. The framework sections comprise—XD Playbook, XD Practices, End2End Design, Development, Operations, Experience, Design Rules, Customer Experience and Business Analyst.

7.4.1   XD Playbook Framework (3.1.2.1)

Guide Notes

XD, as a descriptor, denotes *User Experience Design.*
   XD Playbook denotes the Framework (3.1.2.1) in general. It comprises an overall diagram containing, text, labelled boxes, images, notes, icons and photos (Fig. 7.2). *XD Playbook* is considered to equate to UX Framework (3.1.2.1).

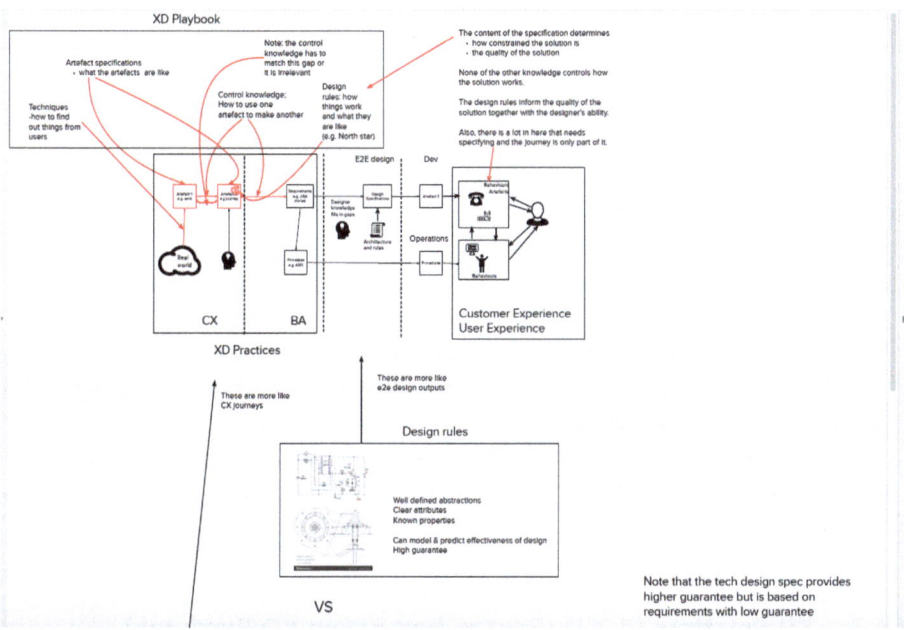

Fig. 7.2   XD playbook framework (3.1.2.1)

7.4.2   XD Playbook (Top Left Rectangular Box)

Guide Notes

Artefact Specification describes what the to-be-designed 'artefact is like'. It is linked to two red-outlined boxes. The left-hand box denotes '*Artefact* 1, e.g. As-Is'. The right-hand box denotes 'Artefact 2, e.g. Journey'.

Techniques describe 'how to find out things from users'. They are subordinate to UX Framework (3.1.2.1) and to UX Practice (2.2.2). *Techniques* are linked to the relation between Artefact 1 and *Real World* within the *Customer Experience* (CX) box.

Control Knowledge describes 'how to use one artefact to make another'.

It is subordinate to UX Framework (3.1.2.1) and UX Practice (2.2.2). It is linked to the relation between *Artefact* 1 and *Artefact 2*. It is also linked to the relation between *Artefact* 2 and '*Requirements*', for example, *JIRA Stories*. JIRA is a requirements management tool for *Agile Methodology*. *Requirements* are called 'stories' having an 'Epic' parent feature.

Note asserts that *Control Knowledge*' has to match the gap (between *Artefact* 1 and *Artefact* 2) or it is irrelevant'. It is linked to the relation between *Artefact* 1 and *Artefact* 2.

Design Rules describe 'how things work and what they are like. North Star is an example.'

Dowell and Long (1989)—see References.

It is subordinate to UX Framework (3.1.2.1) and to UX *Practice* (2.2.2). The descriptor is linked to Artefact 2.

Design Rule Notes assert 'The content of the specification determines:

- how constrained the solution is.
- the quality of the solution.'

The descriptor is subordinate to UX Framework (3.1.2.1) and to UX Practice (2.2.2).

For *Design Rules*—see earlier.

'None of the other knowledge controls how the solution works.'

The *Design Rules* inform the quality of the solution together with the designer's ability.'

For *Design Rules*—see earlier.

'Also, there is a lot in here that needs specifying and the *Journey* is only part of it.'

This is linked by a red line to the *Behaviours* and *Artefacts* box of *Customer/User Experience*.

7.4.3 XD Practices (2.2.1) (Square Box Below XD Playbook)

Guide Notes

XD Practices (equating to UX Practices (2.2.2) are divided into *CX (Customer Experience)* and *BA* (Business Analyst).

XD Practices are linked from the bottom left box, containing 'a Car and a Person Photo' plus

- 'Less well-defined abstractions
- Vague *Attributes*
- Less defined *Properties*
- Cannot model *Effectiveness* of design
- Low guarantee'

The link is labelled 'These are more like *CX journeys*.'

7.4.3.1 CX (Customer Experience)

Guide Notes

Artefact 1 is red line linked to *Artefact 2* red line box. It is also linked to *Real World* cloud icon.

The link is itself labelled 'These are more like *CX journeys*.'

Artefact 2 is linked to Human Head icon. It is also linked to '*Requirements* e.g. *JIRA Stories*', as told by end-users—see *Control Knowledge* earlier.

7.4.3.2 *Business Analyst (BA)*

Artefact 2 is linked to 'Process, for example, Aris' and in turn to 'Design Specifications'. *Artefact 2* is specified in the UX Design Representation (2.3.1). 'Architecture and Rules' are also linked to 'Design Specifications'.

Guide Notes

Artefact 1 denotes the current or 'old' interactive system to be redesigned.

Artefact 2 denotes the future or 'new' interactive system, which is to be designed.

Architecture and Rules denote the nature of an interactive system specification.

Design Specifications denotes the interactive system designs to be implemented.

7.4.4 E2E Design, Dev and Operation

7.4.4.1 E2E (End2End) Design

Guide Notes

Design Specifications are linked to *Requirements*. The descriptor links to UX Design Representation (2.3.1) and is part of UX Framework (3.1.2.1). The link is informed by 'Designer knowledge fill in gaps'. '*Architecture and Rules*' are linked to *Design Specifications*.

7.4.4.2 Dev (Development)

Artefact 2 links *Design Specifications* with '*Behaviours*, Artefacts (plus 'Phone Icon)', which has a two-way link with a Human Icon. Further, linked to the Note: 'Also, there is a lot in here that needs specifying and the journey is only part of it.'

7.4.4.3 Operations

Procedures link from 'Processes, for example, Aris' to Human Icon, which in turn is two-way linked to Person Icon. The descriptor relates to UX Practice (2.2.2) and so to UX Framework (3.1.2.1).

7.4.5 Experience

7.4.5.1 'Customer Experience (Box to the Right of E2E Design, Dev and Operations)

Customer Experience denotes the experience of someone, who buys and consumes products or services typically via websites.

The box contains the '*Behaviours/Artefacts/*'Phone Icon Box, the *Behaviours*/Human Icon Box and the Person Icon'.

7.4.5.2 User Experience' (Box to the Right of E2E Design, Dev and Operations)

Experience denotes the Experience (1.3.2) of people using Human–Computer Technology (1.3.2) to do something as intended and desired.

The box contains the 'Behaviours/Artefacts/'Phone Icon Box, the Behaviours/Human Icon Box and the Person Icon'.

7.4.6 Design Rules (Bottom Rectangular Box)

Design Rules are divided into 2 diagrams and some text, as follows:

- 'Well defined abstractions
- Clear *Attributes*
- Known *Properties*
- Can model and predict *Effectiveness* of design
- High *Guarantee*'

The *Design Rules* are themselves contrasted (as in *VS* for 'versus') with the 'Car and Person Photo Box'. Both boxes relate to the following:

'Note that the tech(nical) design spec(ification) provides higher *Guarantee* but is based on *Requirements* with low *Guarantee*.'

For *Design Rules*—see earlier.

7.4.7 Bottom 3 Columns—CX, BA and E2E

7.4.7.1 CX (Customer Experience)

- 'Persons and channels used
- Timings of events/messages
- Sequence of Events'

CX is part of the UX Framework (3.1.2.1).

7.4.7.2 BA (*Business Analyst*)

- '*Functional Requirements*
- *Process*—happy and unhappy path
- *Data Items*
- *Timings* and *Event Triggers*
- *Operational Design*'

These are part of the UX Design Representation (2.4) (and so of the UX Framework (3.1.2.1).

7.4.7.3 E2E (*End2End*)

- 'Specifications of functions
- Specify sequencing and control
- Data structures and specifications
- Events (technical/data)
- Map design onto architecture'

E2E is part of the UX Design Representation (2.4) and UX Framework (3.1.2.1).

Identical Descriptors

Framework (3.1.2.1)/Practice (2.2.1).

Additional Descriptors

XD/User Experience Design/Artefact Specifications/Artefact/Techniques/Real World/ Control Knowledge/Requirements/JIRA Stories/Note/Design Rules/Notes/XD Practice/ CX Customer Experience/Process/Attributes/Properties/Data Items/Effectiveness/Artefact 1/Artefact 2/Timings/Events Triggers/Operational Design Architecture and Rules/Design/ Specifications/Requirements/Functional Requirements) Procedures/Experience/Customer Experience/User Experience/BA.

Review

Middlemass presents the XD Playbook framework by means of graphics and text. It is fully described at a low level. Notes also provide additional explanation and clarification. There is only a single overlap with the initial UX description. Many additional descriptors, however, are subordinate to the concepts of the latter.

Chapter Review

The source material contributions are presented, as they relate frameworks to framing UX design practice. Chakraborty characterises UX frameworks in terms of frame and framing. He proposes a novel 'product-centric' framework. Timmer's contribution is a UX design for performance framework. The latter includes desired/actual performance and diagnosis/prescription. Last, Middlemass presents the XD Playbook framework by means of graphics and text. It is fully described at a low level. The overlap with the initial UX description is only modest. However, many additional descriptors are identified. The latter exhibit both subordinate and superordinate relations between the initial UX description and the UX source material.

Chapter Carry Forward

The carry-forward from Chaps. 4–10 appears in Appendix 1. It constitutes the basis for the initial UX description and hence for the guide to framing design practice for UX. The appendix is intended to support readers in applying the initial UX description to the UX practitioner source material. Also, in completing the associated exercise assignments. Appendix 1 is not for reading as a text in itself, but for consultation in its application.

7.5   Exercise Assignment

The exercise assignment is intended to test readers' understanding and application of the concepts presented. Also to support tailoring the initial UX description to their own design requirements.

Consulting 7.2–7.4.

- *Check* the shared descriptors between the initial UX description and the UX source material.
- *Do you agree* with the descriptors identified? If not, then
- *Compile* your own list.
- *Justify* your listing.

Consulting 7.2–7.4

Select the least and most developed UX framework from the three presented.

– *Compare* and
– *Contrast* the two UX Frameworks.
– *Use* the more developed framework to enhance the less developed framework.
– *List* your difficulties in so doing. Why might this be so?
– *Select* from the UX literature an additional UX Framework.
– *Compare* and
– *Contrast* it with one of the three UX frameworks presented in the text.
– *List* your difficulties in so doing.
– *Suggest* why this might be so.

7.6   Notes

[1] Science, as a discipline, has the general problem of understanding natural phenomena. Understanding comprises explaining known phenomena and predicting unknown phenomena. Scientific knowledge, such as laws and theories, are acquired and validated to support understanding natural phenomena.
[2] Engineering, as a discipline, has the general problem of designing artefacts. Designing comprises specifying and implementing such artefacts. Engineering knowledge, such as methods and principles, are acquired and validated to support designing artefacts. Scientific knowledge may contribute to engineering knowledge.

Reference

Dowell, J., & Long, J. (1989). Target paper: Conception of the cognitive engineering design problem. *Ergonomics, 41*(2), 126–139.

UX Practitioner Source Material Describing UX Approaches

8

8.1 Introduction

The chapter presents source materials for framing design practice for UX. They take the form of approaches. The same guide summary/review structure of 4.1 is used here. Likewise for the concepts and their relations. To crosscheck the UX contributions with the initial UX descriptors, see Appendix 1.

8.2 Cummaford Source Material (2023)

Summary

Cummaford's source material embodies a best-practice approach to framing UX design practice. The main concepts are outlined.

8.2.1 UX Best-Practice Approach

'Revenue for *Digital Media* and technology in general, and e-commerce in particular, has grown. *Turnover* for *E-commerce* has increased from about £20 billion in 1998 to about £2 trillion per annum globally. Hardly surprising then, that commercial *Best-Practice* has attracted resources, resulting in its development and advancement. Future research needs to take account of how to apply current *Best-Practice* as part of a UX **Approach** (3.1.2.2).

Such changes in *Best-Practice* include:

1. From design for *Usability* to design for **User Experience** (1.3.2).

2. From design methods to *Design Methods*, enhanced by technical advances in data capture, as exemplified by UX *Analytic Tools*, such as Adobe Analytics and Content Square.
3. From simple online *Transaction Testing* to online *Design Funnel Testing*.
4. From simple online *Transaction Testing* to online *AB Testing*.
5. From *Structured Analysis and Design Methods* to *Lean* UX *Design Methods*.
6. From the *Design Problem* to the *Minimum Viable Product* (MVP).
7. From *Process Design Methods* to *Atomic Design Methods*.
8. From individual online *User Testing* to online *Scaled Up User Testing*.'

Guide Notes

UX Approach, (3.1.2.2) as a descriptor, is a general way of doing UX. It is less formal than Framework (3.3.2).

Best-Practice is the subordinate of UX Practice (2.2.2), in turn the subordinate of Practice (2.2.1). It usually denotes best commercial practice, unless otherwise stated.

User Experience (1.3.2) results from user engagement with interactive services or products.

Design Methods are as enhanced by *Technical Advances* in *Data Capture*. They equate to UX Practice (2.2.2) and so contribute to UX Design Representation (2.1.1).

UX *Analytic Tools* support UX Practice (2.2.2).

Design Funnel Testing involves UX techniques to maximise the upselling of services and products. It is subordinate to UX Practice (2.2.2).

AB Testing uses design alternatives to optimise user/customer journeys. It is subordinate to UX Practice (2.2.2). It is a major form of UX *Transaction Testing*.

Lean UX *Design Methods* denote minimal or 'bottom up' design methods. They are subordinate to UX Practice (2.2.2).

Minimum Viable Product equates with Design Solution (1.8.2). It forms part of the UX Representation (2.3.2).

Atomic Design Methods denotes types of method, which are expressed in terms of their elemental parts.

Scaled Up User Testing evaluates the Performance (2.2.1) of many Users (1.1.2) at the same time.

Identical Descriptors

User Experience (1.3.2)/Approach (3.3.2).

Additional Descriptors

Best Practice/User Experience/Design Methods/UX Analytic Tools/Technical Advances/ Data Capture/Design Funnel Testing/AB Testing/Design Problem/Lean UX Methods/ Minimal Viable Product/Atomic Design Methods/Scaled Up User Testing.

Review

Cummaford's proposed changes to best-practice design accommodate the requirements of UX best practice. Only two descriptors overlap with the initial UX description. Other descriptors relate to the description, but only at a lower level of description and not at the level of identity.

8.3   Blyth Source Material (2023)

Summary

Blyth describes HCI practice around the year 2000. The general approach was that of user-centred design (UCD). The 'how' and the 'what' of UCD design practice are characterised.

8.3.1   Rules of Engagement

'For those that entered into the world of *Human-Computer Interaction* at the turn of the century, the *Rules of Engagement* were straightforward: Systems should be engineered to be cognitively ergonomic. They should be usable. What is *Usability*? That was simple too. It was defined by ISO 9241 as allowing users to achieve their goals with '*Effectiveness, Efficiency and Satisfaction.*'

Each of those three terms had a variety of associated metrics. **Practitioners** (1.5.2) at this time duly measured those metrics which ensured their systems were usable. All was well. The ISO standard was well defined, forged in the heat of thorough committee review. It was clear to all its advocates that it was both necessary and sufficient to describe a quality **User Experience** (1.3.2).

While ISO 9241 was the 'what' of *User-Centred Design*, ISO 13407 offered the 'how'. Now in addition to assessing a system's *Usability*, there were reliable and repeatable processes to achieve expected outcomes. Finally, the 'what and the how' could all be understood within broader *Conceptions* of the entire *HCI Discipline*, such at that of Long and Dowell (1989).

With the zeal of the recently converted, the Practitioners (1.5.2) in the Class of 2000 explained (to anyone that they thought needed to hear) that the creation of quality systems really was a simple affair. It was obvious. Follow the processes, place users at the heart of each step, measure for *Effectiveness*, *Efficiency* and *Satisfaction*, and a good result will follow. And woe betide anyone that got in the way of this pure and foolproof logic… with distractions of new technologies, or the realpolitik of limited budgets and time constraints, or—worst of all—patently unverifiable claims of 'but this design is better'.

Guide Notes

Rules of Engagement, as a descriptor, denotes how the *HCI* Practitioner (1.5.2) goes about their Practice (2.2.1).

User-Centred Design (*UCD*) denotes the 'how' of HCI design. The contrast is with computer-centric design, product-centric design or experience-centric. The difference is in the design focus.

Usability is a criterion for the *UCD* design of interactive Human–Computer Technology (1.3.2). An alternative is 'ease-of-use'.

Identical Descriptors

Practitioner (1.5.2)/User Experience (1.3.2).

Additional Descriptors

Rules of Engagement/User-Centred Design/Usability/Effectiveness/Efficiency/Satisfaction.

Review

Blyth is describing HCI Practice around 2000. The time before UX began to take hold. The general approach was that of user-centred design (UCD). The 'how' and the 'what' of UCD design practice are described. Only two descriptors overlap with the initial UX description.

8.4   Sinclair Source Material (2023)

Summary

Sinclair's contribution is taken from a project report. The latter applies a UX heuristics approach to review three flagship phones. The contribution embodies aspects of approach, method and case study. However, only its UX approach is addressed here. Other aspects are addressed elsewhere (11.2). The heuristics applied are explicit and defined, but not further elaborated. The relations between them are not identified. It falls short then of being a framework. Length precludes its complete inclusion.

8.4.1   Executive Summary

'In a nutshell, Samsung scores relatively poorly on the *Marketing Journey*. Whilst the accessories PCD is extremely clear, and scores highest out of the competitors, the *Product Finder* is awkward to use. This is because of issues with the filter, sort and default listing. It therefore scores low on *Effort*, *Generalisation* and *Clarity*.

On the other hand, Samsung scores highest on the *Upsell Journey*. Samsung scores 2: OK, on everything but *Flexibility*.

In general, there are missed opportunities to upsell more products, but the overall journey is straightforward. Improvements can still be made at a more granular level.'

8.4.2   Method

'The accessories-buying process for three different companies were evaluated: Samsung, Apple, and Google. To perform a competitive analysis, each site was judged against the same set of heuristics. Components and pages were judged on a three point scale: 1 = poor, 2 = OK, 3 = good. The method comprises—Competitors, Journeys and Heuristics.'

8.4.3   Competitors

'Three flagship phones were looked at specifically: the Samsung S10, the Apple iPhone X, and the Google Pixel 3. All are high-end, expensive, models and are likely to appeal to a similar *Demographic*. The *Websites* for each product have many similarities, but have their own style.'

8.4.4   Journeys

'For each retailer, there are two main purchase routes for accessories.

Marketing Journey
Accessories are marketed on *PCD* pages and on their own *PDPs*. The User is likely to enter this journey when they are looking directly for accessories and browsing relevant pages.'

Upsell Journey
'Certain accessories are also suggested when the user makes a related purchase. We compared the *Buying Journey* for the Samsung S10, the Apple iPhone X, and the Google Pixel, and evaluated how accessories were upsold for each.'

Guide Notes

Buying Journey describes the customer navigation through the website pages in search of, or in completion of, a purchase. Possible journeys are supported by the UX Design Representation (2.1.2) and are a product of UX Practice (2.2.2).

User Journey describes any type of journey undertaken by the user/human/customer, for example buying, marketing and upsell.

Marketing Journey describes the customer navigation through the website pages exposing a product, such as to encourage its purchase. Possible journeys are supported by the UX Design Representation (2.1.2) and are a product of UX Practice (2.2.2).

Upsell Journey describes the customer navigation through the website pages with a view to purchasing a product.

8.4.5   Heuristics

'The *Heuristics* used in the review follow:

Efficiency... Consistency... Effort... Flexibility... Generalisation... Clarity... Feedback...'

Guide Notes

Heuristics are essentially 'rules of thumb' or 'hints and tips' for doing something—here a UX review or evaluation taking a UX Approach (3.1.2.2). Although defined, they are not guaranteed to be optimal, perfect, or rational. However, they are sufficient for reaching an immediate, short-term goal or approximation. The use of individual *Heuristics* is part of UX Practice (2.2.2) and contributes to the UX Design Representation (2.1.2). This holds for all *Heuristics* listed.

8.4.6   Some Examples from the Review

'*Product Category Detail*

The *PCDs* have a number of variations, in both the order and manner in which content is presented.

1. Navigation Bar

Both Google and Apple use a Navigation Bar. This is at the top of the page before the key visual...'

2. More Items

Samsung has a maximum of 4 categories on the screen whereas both Apple and Google provide more, 8 and 6 respectively, providing greater flexibility and granularity...

3. Placement

Samsung introduces the categories after the key visual…

4. Layout

Apple and Google also have a more varied *Layout*. The elements occupy one, two and three column layouts…

5. Navigation

Apple introduces accessories inline with their iPhone *PCD*… Samsung only introduces accessories at the level above this, the Product Family Showcase…

Summary

Samsung scores relatively poorly on the *Marketing Journey*… Additionally there are major problems with the S10 journey… Apple is surprisingly inconsistent…

Upsell Journeys

Summary

The *Upsell Journey* evaluates how accessories are sold to the user once they choose to buy a flagship phone. The scoring is the opposite of the marketing journey. The Samsung S10 scores highest, Apple iPhone second, and Google Pixel third…'

Guide Notes

Product Category Detail provides information on the product category, as opposed to on the product itself. *PCDs* figure in the UX Design Representation (2.4) and are a product of UX Design Practice (2.2.1).

Identical Descriptors

None.

Additional Descriptors

Buying Journey/User Journey/Marketing Journey/Upsell Journey/Heuristics/Product Category/Efficiency/Consistency/Effort/Flexibility/Generalisation/Clarity/Feedback.

Review

Sinclair's source material applies heuristics to review three phones (Samsung, Apple and Google). It constitutes a UX approach. It is explicit and defined, but not the relations between heuristics. There is no overlap with the initial UX description, in spite of it being a UX project. The descriptor level is almost entirely subordinate to UX design representation and the result of UX design practice.

8.5   Timmer Source Material (2010)

Summary

Timmer proposes a novel framing for UX design practice. It takes the form of a UX engineering approach. The structure is explicit and detailed. The relations between elements are identified. It contrasts with other approaches, such as applied science and innovation. The approach comprises the following sections: Web Site analytics, AB Testing and Design Specifications.

8.5.1   Web Site Analytics

'*Information Architects* design the pages reflected in statistical analyses of the web site. *Web Site Analytics* reflect a limited 'glimpse' of a site design's **Performance** (3.3.1). For example, a business has sales targets for the *Digital Channel*. The current volume level of 10 product sales per day may be insufficient to justify the cost of the channel. *Uplift* is needed to 20 sales per day, to achieve business benefit for maintaining the channel. In the case of the conversion illustration of 6 of the 261 visitors to the *Quote Page*, changes would need to be made to the *Digital Channel* (*Website*) and/or sales process. This is so that a 7.6% conversion rate is attained (20 *Confirmation Pages* are seen from the 261 who saw the *Quote Page*). The latter may be possible without changing the website significantly. For example, a '5% off' promotion could be made to the user.

Alternatively, hypotheses may be formulated as to how the *Quote Page* might be improved. This with a view to getting more people through to click '*Buy Now*' and start filling in the *Personal Details Form*. Instructional text may be insufficient to reassure the user how easy the process is. '*Buy Now*' buttons may be out of sight and require scrolling. The business, in conjunction with the information architect, may thereby seek to redesign parts of the site to achieve improved *Conversion Rates* and *Sales Volume Uplift*.

Alternatively, the business, in conjunction with digital marketers, may place an increasing number of *Banner Adverts* on partner sites. This would be to drive twice the volume of users to the *Product Page*. Thereby mining the existing statistical patterns through the *Conversion Funnel* to reach the same end result. That is 20 target sales for the channel.

Drawing on *Conversion Funnel* data, the website is changed. Maybe with clearer instructional text. Or two '*Buy Now*' buttons, one at the top and one at the bottom of the page. The changed site is then measured, in a similar manner to the first design. Over time a comparative *Conversion Funnel* is generated. While a method of applied science/other method would appear to be employed, the difference between two (measured) digital experiences may be a great number of site alterations. Each alteration reflecting a hypothesis, with many parties within the business generating such hypotheses and requesting changes. If *Uplift* is attained, it may be hard or impossible to know which alteration was most effective. However, all the business wants is *Uplift*, not the practice of a purely scientific/other approach or the associated method'.

Guide Notes

Performance, (3.3.1) describes the effectiveness of an interactive system, expressed as how well the work is performed and at what resource cost to the user.

Web Site Analytics describe the results of the numerical, and often statistical, treatment of data derived about *User Journeys*. Their use is part of UX Practice (2.2.2). They may also be used to support aspects of the UX Design Representation (2.1.2).

Quote Page describes the webpage, which shows the cost of a product or service to the potential purchaser. The page forms part of the UX Design Representation (2.1.1).

Digital Channel is contrasted with non-digital channels, such as retail shop networks. The latter may offer the same or different products and services.

Confirmation Page describes the validation by the User (1.1.2)/customer of the intent and decision to purchase a product or service. The descriptor is embodied in the UX Design Representation (2.1.2) by UX Practice (2.2.2).

Buy Now instantiates the decision of the User (1.1.2)/customer to purchase a product or service. Here, the function is taken by buttons.

Personal Details Form describes the information required from the User (1.1.2)/customer, such that the purchase and its delivery can be effected by the seller. The descriptor is part of the UX Design Representation (2.1.2) by means of UX Practice (2.2.2).

Conversion Rates express the ratio of user/customers, interested in a product or service to those, who actually effect a purchase thereof.

Conversion Funnel describes the means by which *Information Architects* attempt to convert 'warm' user/customers into actual product or service purchasers. Use of the *Conversion Funnel* is part of UX Practice (2.2.2).

(Sales Volume) Uplift describes the actual sales, which result from a particular aspect of UX Design Representation (2.1.2).

Banner Adverts describe general forms of publicity presented on channels other than the one, which offers the product or service for purchase.

Product Page presents information on the product or service, which the channel is putting on offer. It figures as part of the UX Design Representation (2.1.2).

8.5.2   AB Testing

'To compliment multiple design changes to pages, it is possible to conduct *'Split' Testing*, or *AB Testing*. Testing is of page elements such as button designs, labelling, font size, imagery and so forth. In this case, two buttons may be designed, one saying Buy Now, and another saying Join Us. These might be placed on the page in equal measure until a statistical difference in usage is detected. One design may then prevail as more effective.

Testing single hypotheses may also be undertaken. An image of a sick animal may be more effective at driving people to buy pet insurance than an image of a happy customer. The page *Design Specifications* that support the *Conversion Funnel* can in this way be modified. They are thereby optimised to meet business goals. The cost of changing the Digital Channel's **User Experience** (1.3.2) needs to be weighed against incremental gains, through better *Conversion Rates.*

A sketch was presented earlier of the *Conversion Funnel* and a suggestion made that *Web Analytics* might be used to 'optimise' a website. *Web Site Analytics* appear to support *Website* optimisation. But the latter is about more than measuring aggregated and individual click paths'.

Guide Notes

AB Testing evaluates one interface element against another in a real time 'split' test. The descriptor is part of UX Practice (2.2.2) and contributes to UX Design Representation (2.1.2).

Join Us is an alternative to *'Buy Now'* buttons. The descriptor instantiates the decision of the User (1.1.2)/customer to proceed with the purchase of a product or service. Here, the function is taken by a text invitation, rather than a button.

Design Specifications describe the changes to a design, reflecting the results of the application of a *Conversion Funnel*. They constitute a UX Design Representation (2.1.2) and form part of UX Practice (2.2.2).

User Experience (1.3.2) describes, the effect on the User (1.1.2), which results from engagement with interactive systems.

Conversion Rates describe the ratio or percentage of Users (1.1.2) navigating from a *Quote Page* for the cost of a *Product* or a service to the *Confirmation Page*. The navigation, in effect, completes the sale or subscription.

Conversion Funnel describes a User's (1.1.2) navigation towards, and possible achievement of, a goal. It is a common device of UX Internet design. It is the object of UX *Design Practice (2.2.1)* and subordinate to it.

8.5.3   Design Specifications

'Optimisation has a second component, in the form of *Design Specifications*. Behind the aggregated statistics are designed pages that form the User's Experience (1.3.2). To optimise the pages, in line with *Business Targets*, *Design Specifications* are required, and specifically 'designs for Performance' (3.3.1). Designed changes need to attain targets. Also, to address *User Problems* in getting through the *Funnel*. The **User** (1.1.2) can at any point leave the Funnel simply by clicking away on a *Bookmark*. To convert the *Prospective Customer* into a *Business Customer* in the *Digital Channel*, any confusions during the *Purchasing Journey* need to be eliminated from the design. A specification for a *Design Solution* is required, to compliment the *Design Problems* identified by the web site analytics. Together, *Analytics* and *Design Specifications* support *Website Optimisation*.'

Guide Notes

Performance, as a descriptor, see earlier.
  Purchasing Journey describes the User (1.1.2) navigation, required to buy a product or service. It figures in the UX Design Representation (2.1.2).
  Design Problem can be expressed in various ways, for example, the difference between desired and actual Performance (3.3.1). It complements the UX Design Solution (1.8.2).
  Design Solution complements the Design Problem (1.8.2). It can be expressed in different ways, for example, desired and actual Performance (3.3.1) being identical or not. The descriptor figures in the UX Design Representation (2.1.2).

Identical Descriptors

User Experience (1.3.2)/Performance (3.3.1).

Additional Descriptors

Information Architect/Quote Page/Website Analytics/Analytics/Digital Channel/ Confirmation Page/Website/Business Targets/Buy Now/Personal Details Form/Conversion Rates/Conversion Funnel/Sales Volume Uptake/Uplift/Banner Adverts/Product Page/AB Testing/Join Us/Design Specifications/Optimisation/Prospective Customer/Business Customer/Purchasing Journey/Design Problem/Design Solution.

Review

Timmer proposes a novel framing for UX design practice in the form of a UX engineering approach. It contrasts with other approaches, such as craft and applied science. The approach is based on an engineering conception of HCI. It comprises of web site analytics, AB testing and design specifications. There is only a two descriptor overlap with the initial UX description.

Chapter Review

Source materials are presented. They describe approaches for framing UX design practice. Cummaford's proposed changes to best-practice design accommodate the requirements of UX best practice. Blyth describes HCI practice around the year 2000. The general approach was that of user-centred design (UCD). Sinclair's approach applies heuristics to review three phones (Samsung, Apple and Google). Timmer proposes a novel framing for UX design practice in the form of a UX engineering approach. The approach is based on an engineering conception of HCI.

Chapter Carry Forward

The carry-forward from Chaps. 4–10 appears in Appendix 1. It constitutes the basis for the initial UX description and hence for the guide to framing design practice for UX. The appendix is intended to support readers in applying the initial UX description to the UX practitioner source material. Also, in completing the associated exercise assignments. Appendix 1 is not for reading as a text in itself, but for consultation in its application.

8.6   Exercise Assignment

The exercise assignment is intended to test readers' understanding and application of the concepts presented. Also to support tailoring the initial UX description to their own design requirements.

Consulting 8.2–8.5

– *Check* the shared descriptors between the initial UX description and the UX source material.
– *Do you agree* with the descriptors identified? If not, then
– *Compile* your own list.
– *Justify* your listing.

Consulting 8.2–8.5

– *Select* two UX approaches from the three presented.
– *Compare* and
– *Contrast* the two UX approaches.
– *Use* the more developed approach to enhance the less developed approach.
– *List* your difficulties in so doing.

– *Why* might this be so?

Consulting 8.2–8.5

– *Select* the approach having the most potential to become a framework. Select a framework from 7.2 to 7.4 having the most potential for enhancing an approach.
– *Apply* the former to the latter.
– *List* your difficulties in so doing.
– *Why* might this be so?

– *Select* from the UX literature an additional UX approach.
– *Compare* and
– *Contrast* it with one of the three UX approaches presented here.
– *List* your difficulties in so doing.
– *Why* might this be so?

Reference

Long, J., & Dowell, J. (1989). Conceptions of the discipline of HCI: Craft, applied science and engineering. In A. Sutcliffe, & L. Macaulay (Eds), *People and computers V*. Cambridge University Press.

UX Practitioner Source Material Describing UX Methods

9

9.1 Introduction

The chapter presents source materials for framing design practice for UX. They take the form of methods. The same guide summary/review structure of 4.1 is used here. Likewise for the concepts and their relations. To crosscheck the UX contributions with the initial UX descriptors, see Appendix 1.

9.2 Cummaford Source Material (2023)

Summary

Cummaford proposes a UX best-**Practice** (3.3.1) methodology, based on UX best-practice. The sections comprise—Changes to Best-Practice, Mapping of Best-Practice and E-Commerce Systems.

9.2.1 UX Best Practice Method

'Revenue for *Digital Media* and technology in general, and *E-Commerce* in particular, has grown. *Turnover* for *E-Commerce* has increased from about £20 billion in 1998 to about £2 trillion per annum globally. Hardly surprising then, that commercial *Best-Practice* has attracted resources, resulting in its development and advancement. Future *Research* needs to take account both of how to apply current *Best-Practice* in the acquisition of *HCI Engineering Design Principles* and what format best suits their application to current *Best-Practice* design.'

© The Author(s), under exclusive license to Springer Nature Switzerland AG 2025
J. Long, *Guide to Framing Design Practice for UX*, Synthesis Lectures
on Human-Centered Informatics, https://doi.org/10.1007/978-3-031-68981-9_9

Guide Note

Best-Practice, as a descriptor, is the subordinate of UX Practice (2.2.2), in turn the subordinate of Practice (2.2.1). The *Best-Practice* frequency of occurrence suggests its inclusion in the final UX Description.

9.2.2 Changes to Best-Practice

'To the latter ends, the changes to *Best-Practice*, since the completion of the *Research*, are identified and implications for *Best-Practice* and for *HCI Engineering Design Problems* application format noted. Future UX *Research* would do well to take account of both sets of implications. Such required changes in *Best-Practice* follow:

1. 'From design for *Usability* to design for UX (**User Experience** (1.3.2)).'

Guide Notes

UX denotes design for User Experience (1.3.2).

    User Experience (1.3.2) denotes the User (1.1.2) state resulting from successful UX *Design*. Note that User-Centred Design can also design for *User Experience* (1.3.2) as in experience-centred design (ECD). Likewise, UX can design for *Usability*.

2. 'From Design Methods to *Design Methods*, enhanced by technical advances in *Data Capture*. For example, UX *Analytic Tools*, such as Adobe Analytics and Content Square.'

Guide Notes

Design Methods constitute the methodological design or 'how' knowledge supporting design. They contrast with substantive/declarative or 'what' design knowledge such as models.

    UX *Analytic Tools* are a relatively recent development in interactive systems design support. They constitute a form of encapsulated UX knowledge supporting *Design Methods*.

3. 'From simple *Online Transaction Testing* to *Online Design Funnel Testing*.'

Guide Note

Online Design Funnel Testing is a basic UX Method (3.1.2.3). *Conversion Funnel* describes a user's navigation towards, and possible achievement of, a goal. It is referenced by a number of source material contributions.

4. 'From simple *Online Transaction Testing* to *Online 'AB' Testing.'*

Guide Note

Online AB Testing is a basic UX Method (3.1.2.3). Two designs are tested simultaneously in real time and the results compared.

5. 'From *Structured Analysis and Design Methods* to *'Lean* UX' Design Methods (3.1.2.3).'

Guide Note

Lean UX *Design Methods* denote 'bottom up' or 'cut down' methods. The term 'lean' predates the UX Movement (1.4.2) and was used in contrast to *Structured Analysis and Design methods.*

6. 'From the *Design Problem to the Minimum Viable Product (MVP).'*

Guide Note

Minimum Viable Product (*MVP*) equates to the UX *Design Solution.* This is to the extent that UX *Design Problem* and *User Requirements* relate to UX *Design Solutions. User Requirements* are much referenced in the UX literature. They appear to have some traction within UX. The descriptor is considered for inclusion in the final UX description.

7. 'From *Process Design Methods* to *Atomic Design Methods.'*

Guide Notes

Process Design Methods include *Structured Analysis and Design Methods* (see earlier), as well as *Design Methods* more generally. *Process Design Methods* are subordinate to UX Practice (2.2.2).

   Atomic Design Methods contrast with *Process Design Methods* by way of their differing descriptors and elemental components. The latter have attained some popularity among UX Practitioners (1.5.2).

8. 'From *Individual Online User Testing* to *Online 'Scaled Up' User Testing.'*

Note that in all cases, the full range needs to be included.'

Guide Note

Online Scaled Up User Testing is subordinate to *Online Transaction Testing*. Initially, such testing was individual and offline. *Individual Online Testing* tests more than one user at a time. The actual numbers of users tested can be very large, which speeds up the process.

9.2.3   Mapping of Best-Practice

'All these *Best-Practice* changes can be recruited to the *Design Practice*, used in the **Case Study** (3.1.2.4), to support the acquisition and validation of *HCI Engineering Design Problems*. Such application, however, would necessarily require the mapping of the novel change concepts, such as '*Lean*' and *Minimum Viable Product* to those of the conception, such as *Design Problem* and *Design Solution* and, indeed, *HCI-Engineering Design Problem*. The Format of the latter for *Best-Practice* application was an issue at the time of the *Research* and remains one now.'

Guide Note

Best-Practice implicates UX *Best-Practice*. In contrast, for example, with UCD or more generally HCI *Best-Practice*. UX *Best-Practice* is at the same level of description as UCD and subordinate to HCI. UX and UCD *Best-Practice* are in turn subordinate to Practice (2.2.1) and to UX Practice (2.2.2).

   Best-Practice Changes embody developments/advancements and so changes to *Best-Practice*. The same or similar comments apply to both.

9.2.4   E-Commerce Systems

'In conclusion, as concerns *E-Commerce Systems*, it is clear, that they were a promising area of *Research*, in terms of their potential for commercial development. The selection of *Physical Goods* E-Commerce Transaction Systems has also proven to be an area of commercial interest and success. There is no shortage of such systems, with Amazon emerging as perhaps the best known, and possibly biggest. *Information E-Commerce Systems*, however, have almost disappeared in the form characterised in Cycle 2 development. The general class-level description of transaction systems for information may still be valid, for example, the sale of *Virtual Goods* in games or the *Metaverse*, but *SMS News Alert Services* as such hardly exist. However, the particular example is less important than the development of the *HCI Engineering Design Principle Conception* and the *Class-based Approach* themselves.'

Guide Note

E-Commerce Systems are of major importance to UX, which cannot be overestimated. They will increase as high-street sales outlets reduce. Both are causally related. Such systems are a subordinate of Human–Computer Technology (1.3.2).

Identical Descriptors

User Experience (1.3.2)/Case Study (3.1.2.4)/Practice (3.3.1).

Additional Descriptors

Digital Media/E-Commerce/Turnover/Best-Practice/UX/HCI Engineering Design Principles/Data Capture/User Experience/HCI Engineering Design Problems/Design Method/ UX Analytic Tools/Design Problem/Design Solution/Research/Usability Online Design Funnel Testing/Online AB Testing/Lean UX Design Methods/Minimum Viable Product (MVP)/Process Design Methods/Online Scaled up User testing/Best-Practice/E-Commerce Systems.

Review

Cummaford's source material presents a methodology for UX best-practice. There is a three descriptor overlap with the initial UX description. A range of additional descriptors are identified. Most are relational with the UX description, but at a lower level of description.

9.3 Grant Source Material (2023)

Summary

Grant uses a user centred design (UCD) approach to framing design practice. Implicated is a method, expressed as a set of UCD steps. Although not described as UX, it can be easily tailored for UX application. For that reason, it is included here. It also illustrates the overlap between UCD and UX.

9.3.1 UCD Steps Method

'The contribution uses the steps from BS EN ISO 9241-210 as a broad **Approach** (3.1.2.2) for Framing Design **Practice** (3.3.1). Most notably to understand the *Context of Use*, specify the *User Requirements*, produce *Design Solutions*, and evaluate the design until a fit-for-purpose solution is found. For each of these steps, specific Approaches (3.3.1) that work are used.'

Guide Notes

Approach (3.3.1), as a descriptor is superordinate to UX Approach (3.1.2.2) and to UX method (3.1.2.3).

Practice (3.3.1) appears along with framing design Practice (3.3.1) in the form of Methods (3.1.2.3).

Design Solution describes the outcome of solving a design problem. It forms part of the Design Representation (2.1.1). It also relates to expressions of Performance (2.2.1).

9.3.1.1 Context of Use/User Requirements

'For *Context of Use Analysis*, *Cognitive Work Analysis* is applied and in particular the *Contextual Activity Template*. The latter maps out all the system's functions and the different situations that end-users encounter. Also, *Tabular Task Analysis* is applied. The latter expresses the user's tasks in the subject-verb-object format. The format was used initially after seeing the sentence structure outlined in the book 'Guidelines for Developing Instructions' by Kay Inaba et al. (2004). It turned out to be a useful approach to *Task Analysis*. A template was created in Excel that divides up the elements of a user's tasks in this way.

The Approach (3.3.1) allows development of *Task Analysis* in a consistent and systematic manner. At this stage, a record of an inventory of all the system's elements is created. For interactive Systems, this involves recording each user interface screen and element. The Approach (3.1.1.2) accumulates large amounts of data, which have then to be reduced as needed.'

Guide Notes

Context of Use describes the situation in which Users (1.1.2) perform work. It includes any aspects (physical or mental), which exert an influence on the worker and so on Performance (2.2.1). The descriptor is part of the Scope (1.8.2) of Approach (3.3.1). It is a part of the Design Representation (2.1.1).

Task Analysis reflects task activity and associated behaviour. It is superordinate to *Cognitive Work Analysis*. Results figure in parts of the Design Representation (2.1.1).

9.3.1.2 User Requirements

'To understand *User Requirements*, the relevant Human Factors parameters are applied to the *Context of Use*. Spreadsheets are compiled that contain *Principles, Patterns, Guidelines* etc. The source is recorded, a link to the source where applicable, and the key insights from the source. Also included are keywords for which to search. This allows filter and search for *Patterns* across the data collected. It is a '*Commonplace*' *Book*. Any source of evidence is noted, if of help. Large numbers of *Principles, Patterns*, and *Guidelines* are applied. It is then a case of applying the right parameters to the situation.'

Guide Notes

User Requirements describe the needs/wants/wishes/hopes of the User (1.1.2). The latter as concerns a change in Human–Computer Technology (1.3.2), with which they will have to interact. It forms part of the Design Representation (2.1.1).

Principles describe a type of design knowledge. They support Frameworks (3.1.2.1) and Approaches (3.1.2.2). They determine Design Representations (2.1.1).

Patterns describe commonly recurring elements of different UX Design Solutions (1.8.2) to the same UX Design Problem (1.8.2). They form part of a Framework (3.1.2.1) or Approach (3.1.2.2). They determine Design Representations (2.1.1).

Guidelines describe 'rules of thumb' or 'hints and tips' for good design. They support Frameworks (3.1.2.1) and Approaches (3.1.2.2). They determine Design Representations (2.1.1).

9.3.1.3 Design Solutions

'Concerning the production of *Design Solutions*, a range of options is first identified. Then prototypes for different possible solutions. For example, PowerPoint to simulate Interactive User Interfaces. The contribution favours how IDEO's CEO Brown talks about the need to 'build to think.' Also, the 'fail faster to succeed sooner' approach.

Concerning the evaluation of *Design Solutions*, each proposed *Design Solution* is assessed against the parameters identified earlier. For example, this might involve assessment against clauses from *Standards*, such as consistency of the positioning of controls. It might also involve **Performance** (3.3.1)-related parameters, such as task completion rates. Also collecting subjective, but quantifiable *Feedback* from users, acquired by means of the *Single Ease Question* and the *System Usability Scale*. Qualitative Feedback from users might also be collected.'

Guide Notes

Design Solutions are to be contrasted with UX Design Problems (1.8.2). The latter imply Performance (3.3.1) is not as desired (usually less). The former imply that Performance (3.3.1) is as desired.

Standards describe the prescriptions for effective design. They may form part of a Framework (3.1.2.1) and an Approach (3.1.2.2). They can determine Design Representations (2.1.1).

Performance (3.3.1) expresses how well work is performed. Also, at what resource cost to the user.

Identical Descriptors

Approach (3.1.2.2)/Practice (3.3.1)/Performance (3.3.1).

Additional Descriptors

Context of Use/User Requirements/Task Analysis/Principles/Patterns/Guidelines/Design Solutions/Standards/Single Ease Question/System Usability Scale/User Requirements/ Commonplace Book/Cognitive Work Analysis.

Review

Grant's framing of design practice includes a method, expressed as a set of UCD steps. The scope of the latter comprises context of use, user requirements and design solutions. The initial UX descriptors are subordinate to more general ones. There is a three descriptor overlap with the initial UX description.

9.4   Middlemass Source Material (2023)

Summary

Middlemass' contribution embodies a UX method, supported by a framework. Only the method is described here. The latter's sections comprise—Reporting Lines, Tools and Notations, Product, Happy Path Processes, Best Practice and Design Needs.

9.4.1   XD (Experience Design)

'Some notes from the coalface: for the last few years I've been back in the *Experience Fold* and am in a team currently known as 'XD' for *Experience Design* ('currently' because we spend more time in reorganisations than in a stable structure!).'

Guide Notes

Experience Fold, as a descriptor, is novel. Ignoring any intended or unintended ironic association with sheep, *Fold* could be a candidate alternative to the *UX* descriptor Movement (1.4.2) (also field of study and community). It is retained for future consideration as such.

   Experience Design (XD) is much like UX Practice (2.2.2). XD is used here to qualify a type of organisational arrangement, as well as its usual meaning. The use is appropriate. The contributor's dash of irony here should be noted, enjoyed and taken seriously.

9.4.2   Reporting Lines

'Rearranging *Reporting Lines* is guaranteed to solve all possible *Problems*. Anyway, *Experience Design* is supposed to indicate a combination of *Customer Experience* and *Colleague Experience* but in practice it's much more of the latter and less of the former.'

Guide Notes

Reporting Lines communicate with another, above or below them. The communication is for the purpose of executing or discharging work responsibilities. *Management* is typically involved at one or more levels. The use here is no doubt ironic, but the issue is serious. Many problems are implicated. *Reporting Lines* and management are involved in trying to solve such problems. UX designers, like other staff, are inevitably involved in the address of such problems.

   Problems are not well specified. The meaning appears to be very inclusive. At least, it is not considered to be limited to User Experience Problems (1.5.2).

   Experience Design comprises both *Customer Experience* and *Colleague Experience*. Both are subordinate to User Experience (1.3.2).

9.4.3   Tools and Notations

'In reality, most of the team are *Business Process* designers and much of the *Work* is done using a *Tool* called 'ARIS' which uses a fairly widely used *Notation* called BPMN (*Business Process Modelling Notation*). Unfortunately it's such a cumbersome *Tool* that a lot of design decisions are made to suit whatever is expedient given the limitations of the *Tool* and the *Notation*! Interestingly, UX is treated as a separate 'add on' to CX.'

Guide Notes

Business Process is much used in UX and especially the concept of business. The latter covers everything from budgetary financing to advertising and to special offers. *Business Process* includes UX, but in different ways. Locating UX appropriately is part of its current challenge.

   Tool supports the conduct of work and can vary in its level of description. At its most general, it is superordinate to Human–Computer Technology (1.3.2). At a lower level of description, it is subordinate to the latter, as in the case of the ARIS *Tool*. Such tools embody knowledge to support design.

   Notation is instantiated here as BPMN (*Business Process Modelling Notation*). It is subordinate to *Business Process*. It is used to express knowledge to support design.

9.4.4 Product

'We've also got an interesting *Practice* whereby the whole *Customer Experience* is reinvented for each product that launches, but as its so difficult to change anything it turns out to be pretty much the same each time, or to have minor variations for each product that just create confusion.'

Guide Notes

Again, note the irony here. However, far from detracting from the point at issue, it actually expresses the underlying frustration, associated with it.

    Practice (3.3.1), as a descriptor denotes UX Practice (2.2.2).

    Customer Experience is subordinate to Experience (1.2.2). It is an alternative to human experience, to User Experience (1.2.2) and to consumer experience. The difference between these types of experience is a matter of much debate among UX Practitioners (1.5.2). This is confirmed by a number of source material contributions.

9.4.5 Happy Path Processes

'Consequently, most of the team is kept so busy continually reinventing the wheel there is hardly any time left to improve anything. I'm fortunate to be working on a more 'green field' project where we have a bit more latitude, but at this stage of the game that largely involves designing very simple '*Happy Path*' processes then tracing individual data items through them to make sure **Users** (1.1.2) are going to be presented with the right bits to do their job—not as straightforward as you might imagine, because adding an attribute into a System Interface is a bit of an undertaking.'

Guide Notes

Happy Paths characterises the user navigation journeys, which are deemed successful for the attainment of the User (1.1.2)/human, customer/consumer goals. As such, they relate to Intend (1.3.2), as a descriptor.

    Users (1.1.2) are interpreted generally here, rather than, for example, as *UX* User (1.1.2). 'Doing the job' might or might not involve UX, depending on the definition of the latter in terms of Conscious Events (1.2.2) or Knowledge and Skills (1.2.2).

9.4.6 Best-Practice

'Even identifying which attribute is required can involve significant work—we recently required one called '*Port Speed*' and were excited to discover the *Product Data Model* contained several similarly named attributes with no indication of which was which. That said, the benefit of being on this project is that we're less constrained in how we're working and free to model things in whatever way fits what the system designers want to know. The wider team, especially managers, have the notion that they should be establishing 'Best-Practice', which generally involves attempting to use whatever document has been well received on a single project (usually only because someone put a lot of work into it) as a template and then wondering why the next project struggles to use it on a slightly different problem.'

Guide Notes

Port Speed is a subordinate of *Data Item*.

Product Data Model constitutes a representation of something for a purpose. Here, *Model* represents product data for the purpose of design. *Model* representation can take many forms.

Best-Practice is not currently part of the initial UX description. However, it is clearly finding popularity among UX Practitioners (1.5.2). This is indicated by a number of other source material contributions. It should be considered for inclusion.

9.4.7 Design Needs

'I've reminded them of the maxim that 'if all you have is a hammer, everything looks like a nail', but it doesn't seem to sink in. It also doesn't appear that there has ever been any work done to find out what the *Recipients of Our Designs* need—they usually just wait for us to produce the first draft and then ask us to add whatever they think is missing and claim that it has always done that way, was due months ago and has been holding them up!'

Guide Note

Recipients of Our Designs are normally called Humans/Users (1.1.2)/Customers/Consumers.

Identical Descriptors

Users (1.1.2).

Additional Descriptors

ExperienceFold/ExperienceDesignXD/ReportingLines/Problems/Experience/Business Practices/Tool/Notation/Work/Practice/CustomerExperience/HappyPathProcess/Users/Port Speed/Model/Product Data Model/Best-Practice/Recipients of Our Designs/Business Process Modelling Notation.

Review

For Middlemass, experience is critical to design practice. However, there are limitations to its specification and implementation. They may relate to the needs of reporting lines, design tools and notations and product launch reinvention. Happy paths design is characterised. There is only a single descriptor overlap with the initial UX description.

Chapter Review

Source contributions of experienced UX practitioners are presented, as they relate to methods for framing UX design practice. Cummaford's source material presents a methodology for a UX best-practice. Grant's framing of design practice includes a method, expressed as a set of UCD steps. For Middlemass, experience is critical to design practice. However, there are limitations to its specification and implementation. The initial UX description is applied to the methods as part of the process of constructing a final feature space.

Chapter Carry Forward

The carry-forward from Chaps. 4–10 appears in Appendix 1. It constitutes the basis for the initial UX description and hence for the guide to framing design practice for UX. The appendix is intended to support readers in applying the initial UX description to the UX practitioner source material. Also, in completing the associated exercise assignments. Appendix 1 is not for reading as a text in itself, but for consultation in its application.

9.5   Exercise Assignment

The exercise assignment is intended to test readers' understanding and application of the concepts presented. Also to support tailoring the initial UX description to their own design requirements.

Consulting 9.2 to 9.4

- *Check* the shared descriptors between the initial UX description and the UX source material.
- *Do you agree* with the descriptors identified? If not, then
- *Compile* your own list.
- *Justify* your listing.

Consulting 9.2 to 9.4

- *Select* two UX Methods from the three presented.

- *Compare* and
- *Contrast* the two UX Methods.
- *Use* the more developed method to enhance the less developed approach.
- *List* your difficulties in so doing.
- *Why* might this be so?

- *Select* from the UX literature an additional UX Method.
- *Compare* and
- *Contrast* it with one of the three UX Methods presented here.
- *List* your difficulties in so doing.
- *Why* might this be so?

Reference

Inaba, K., Parsons, S.O., Smillie, R.M. (2004). https://api.taylorfrancis.com.

UX Practitioner Source Material Describing UX Case Studies

10

10.1 Introduction

The chapter presents source contributions to framing design practice for UX. They take the form of case studies. The same guide summary/review structure of 4.1 is used here. Likewise for the concepts and their relations. To crosscheck the UX contributions with the initial UX descriptors, see Appendix 1.

10.2 Sinclair Source Material (2023)

Summary

Sinclair's contribution is taken from a project case study report. It reviews three flagship 'phones and describes the 'phone accessories marketing and upsell journeys. The review structure constitutes a framing for UX reporting. Only the section headings are listed, along with minimal information, required to understand and apply them in the work assignment. For further details concerning the project see 8.4.'

1. Executive Summary

'In a nutshell, Samsung scores relatively poorly on the *Marketing Journey*. On the other hand, Samsung scores highest on the *Upsell Journey*. In general there are missed opportunities to upsell more products.

2. Method

The accessories-buying process for three different companies were evaluated. Each site was judged against the same set of *Heuristics*.

– Competitors

The three flagship phones were Samsung S10, Apple iPhone X, and Google Pixel 3.

– *Journeys*

For each retailer, there are two main purchase routes for accessories.
   Marketing Journey and *Upsell Journey.*

3. Heuristics

Example *Heuristic—Feedback—*The system should let users know when an action has been performed.

4. Some Examples from the Review

Product Category Detail/Product Finder/Product Detail/Page/Checkout/Landing Pages.

5. Marketing Journeys

Landing Pages/Product Filter/Checkout.

6. Upsell Journeys

Specific Landing Page/Buy Page/Configure Purchase/Buy Page/Checkout.'

Guide Notes

Marketing Journey, as a descriptor, denotes the customer navigation through the website pages exposing a product, such as to encourage its purchase. The UX Design Representation (2.1.1) specifies possible journeys.

   Upsell Journey describes the customer navigation through the website pages with a view to purchasing a product. The UX Design Representation (2.1.2) specifies possible journeys.

   Heuristics are essentially 'rules of thumb' or 'hints and tips' for UX review or evaluation. They contribute to UX Practice (2.2.2).

Identical Descriptors

None.

Additional Descriptors

Marketing Journey/Upsell Journey/Heuristics/Feedback/Product Filter/Product Category Detail/Product Finder/Product Detail/Page/Checkout/Landing Pages/Specific Landing Page/Buy Page/Configure Purchase/Buy Page/Checkout.

Review

Sinclair's case study is summarised. It reviews three flagship 'phones.' Their 'phone accessories marketing and upsell journeys are described. Only the section headings are listed, along with minimal information, required to understand and to apply them in the work assignment. There is no descriptor overlap with the initial UX description.'

10.3   Sinclair Source Material (2023)

Summary

Sinclair's contribution is taken from the case study report of a project to improve the user experience of buying domestic appliances from a major supplier. This entailed reconciling two different Internet sitemaps.

10.3.1 Project

'The project goal was to improve the **User Experience** (1.3.2) for domestic appliances by a major supplier. This entailed reconciling two *Sitemaps*, one from the *Product Team* and one from *SEO Specialists*. Creating new pages to house *Search Engine Content* and refining existing *Page Types* to improve *Engagement* and the *User Journey*. Finally taking a product finder from one *National Site* and refactoring it for another. The work delivered the following *Assets*—a new *Sitemap*, an *AEM Prototype* and a *Virtual Assistant*, to be tested with users in Laboratory-based sessions.'

Guide Notes

User Experience (1.3.2) is primary. The improvement here concerns the online sales of domestic appliances, such as refrigerators and pots and pans.

   Sitemaps support the documentation of *User Journey* across the website. They are part of UX Practice (2.2.2).

   Search Engine Content describes the UX-designed pages, intended to influence the *User Journey*.

Page Types describe the pages designed by the UX design team, which are intended to influence the *User Journey*.

Engagement describes a type of User Experience (1.3.2). It relates to the commitment of the user to the purchase of domestic appliances.

User Journey, as a descriptor, describes how the user navigates the site to achieve their goals, in this case the purchase of domestic appliances. For example, they may explore the site initially to gather general information on refrigerators, because their own has broken down and cannot be repaired. The user may then go on to explore, in detail and at length, refrigerators within their budget, space and delivery requirements. Last, they may add the refrigerator to their trolley and finally activate the *Buy Now Button*.

Assets describe the outputs of UX Practice (2.2.2). In this case, they are a new *Sitemap*, a *Prototype* and a *Virtual Assistant*.

10.3.2 Methodology

15 participants were recruited for a lab-based *Usability Study*. Sessions were organised into three sets, so providing time for findings from one set to be fed into the design and tested in the next set.

Sample and *Equipment*—the 15 *Participants* were... split between male and female, urban and rural, ages 20–65...

Lab equipment comprised various devices, including Desktop Windows Mid range tower + screen etc.

Sessions—the sessions ran for 1 h and were split into three parts; an *Open-ended Interview*, *Prototype* testing and a *Tree Test.'*

Guide Note

Usability Study denotes a way of evaluating how easy technology is to use. It contrasts with focus group for the same purpose.

10.3.3 Testing

'*Prototype* testing ran 25–30 min. The *Scenario* discovered during the interview was used to test the *Prototypes*...

Additional *Scenarios* were given when time permitted...'

All video and recordings were stopped for the Tree Test. It was run on a desktop computer and self-administered and the *Data Capture* was automated...'

For analysis the *Qualitative Data* were printed and were reviewed to identify repeated ideas, issues or findings. These were then tagged with codes or themes. They were then grouped into categories, which form the backbone of this report.'

As concerns the *Prototype,* its primary functions were to accommodate the new *Sitemap,* improve users' *Engagement* with content and facilitate the *User's Journey* through the category hierarchy...'

Guide Notes

Sitemap supports the documentation of User (1.1.2) *Journey* across the website. They are part of the UX Practice (2.2.2).

Engagement describes a type of User Experience (1.2.2). It relates to the commitment of the user to the purchase of domestic appliances.

User Journey describes how the user navigates the site to achieve their goals, in this case the purchase of domestic appliances. For example, they may explore the site initially to gather general information on refrigerators, because their own has broken down and cannot be repaired. The user may then go on to explore, in detail and at length, refrigerators within their budget, space and delivery requirements. Last, they may add the refrigerator to their trolley and finally activate the Buy Now Button.

10.4 Summary Findings

'(Each based on 3 iterations)

Concerning *Product Category Detail (PCD)* a number of participants would not scroll down the page. The first barrier was the size of the key visual....

Images were hugely important to grab participants' attention and identify the content. The lack of suitable *Images* in V1 created a barrier to *Engagement*....

Concerning the *Search Landing Page (SLP)* most participants did not interact with feature benefits when they were presented in a *Carousel.* The *Carousel* was generally missed.....Headings and images were scanned, but sub-headings and descriptions were missed or ignored....

Concerning the *Product Detail Page (PDP)* at this stage of the *User Journey, Features* and *Benefits* were not very useful. *Participants* relayed that they had already seen this type of content. *Participants* responded well to 'How it stacks up.... Most *Participants* tended to focus on the *Product Specification*....'

As concerns navigation, creating a series of *Pages* the user could identify and navigate was a challenge.... The results are acceptable, but disappointing as the minimum requirement is to ensure that users are aware of the options available to them.

Concerning the *Virtual Assistant* the *Virtual Assistant Prototype* was developed from a live example. A new *National Model* was evaluated via *Expert Review* and *Ad-Hoc User Testing.* From the issues uncovered, the decision was made to develop a *Bespoke Version* for the *National Market,* keeping the good and addressing the issues....

The *Progress Meter* was the primary mechanism for moving between choices, rather than the *Next* and *Previous Buttons*.

With the second iteration, the results were still the main focus on the desktop....'

Guide Notes

Product Category Detail Page (PCD), as a descriptor, shows detailed information on types of item for sale. For example, refrigerators as opposed to an individual brand of refrigerator. The contrast is with *Product Detail Page*.

Engagement describes a type of User Experience (1.2.2). It relates to the commitment of the User (1.1.2) to the purchase of domestic appliances.

Search Landing Page (SLP) describes a location on a *Customer Journey*.

Product Detail Page (PDP) shows detailed information on individual products, as opposed to categories of *Products*.

Review is an analytic assessment, typically conducted by 'experts' of different sorts. *Review* can be of any design stage. It is generally quicker, but less effective than participant testing.

Ad Hoc *Testing* contrasts with systematic testing, for example as in the case of lab-based usability testing. Its use is to focus on particular design problems, particularly ones overlooked earlier.

Identical Descriptors

User Experience (1.3.2).

Additional Descriptors

User Experience/Sitemap/Search Engine Content/Page Types/Prototype/Virtual Assistant/ Engagement/User Journey/Assets/Usability Study/Virtual Assistant/Tree Test/Scenarios/ Experience/Product Category Detail (PCD)/Search Landing Page (SLP)/Customer Journey/Product Detail Page (PDP)/Review/Ad Hoc Testing/Progress Meter/Next Button/Previous Button/Participants/SEO Specialist/Product Specification/National Model/ National Site/Products/Bespoke Version/Pages/Review.

Review

Sinclair's source material reports the case study of a project to improve the user experience of buying domestic appliances from a major supplier. This entailed reconciling two different sitemaps. Testing and prototyping are reported. There is a single overlap with the initial UX description.

Chapter Review

UX source material comprises two case studies—both by Sinclair. The first reviews three flagship 'phones. Their accessories marketing and upsell journeys are described. The second reports a project to improve the user experience of buying domestic appliances from a major supplier. This entailed reconciling two different sitemaps, including their testing and prototyping. The case studies frame UX design practice in the form of case study reports.

10.5   Exercise Assignment

The exercise assignment is intended to test readers' understanding and application of the concepts presented. Also to support tailoring the initial UX description to their own design requirements.

Consulting 10.2–10.3.

- *Check* the shared descriptors between the initial UX description and the UX source material.
- *Do you agree* with the descriptors identified? If not, then
- *Compile* your own list.
- *Justify* your listing.

Consulting 10.2–10.3.

- *Select* a UX case study from the literature.
- *Compare* and
- *Contrast* the literature case study with the one presented here.
- *Use* the more detailed case study to enhance the less detailed case study.
- *List* your difficulties in so doing.
- *Why* might this be so?

- *Select* an additional case study from the UX literature.
- *Compare* and
- *Contrast* it with the two UX case studies presented here.
- *List* your difficulties in so doing.
- *Why* might this be so?

Final Description for Framing UX Design Practice

11

11.1 Final UX Description—Rationale and Conventions

The final UX description adopts the following conventions, each based on an associated rationale, which precedes them.

11.1.1 Overlap Between Initial and Final UX Descriptions

The rationale requires identification of the extent of the overlap of descriptors between the initial UX description and the UX practitioner source material. Major overlap would suggest that the levels of description are comparable. They would need little or no modification of their relationship for application. Minor overlap, however, would suggest a mismatch between the levels of description. Comparability would require decreasing the level of description of the initial UX description. Alternatively, increasing the level of description of the UX practitioner source material. Or a conjoint option modifying both levels.

The convention adopts the descriptor overlap between the initial UX description and the UX practitioner source material be identified in **Bold** with the initial letter in upper case. For example, **User** and **Human-Computer Technology**, The criterion for inclusion is a single reference. More and different references, however, might be required for other kinds of study, such as UCD (User-Centred Design) or ECD (Experience-Centred Design).

The following points suggest themselves.

First, the overlap between the initial UX description and the UX source material is only modest.

Second, the overlap could be increased by decreasing the level of description of the initial UX description, increasing the level of the UX source material or both.

© The Author(s), under exclusive license to Springer Nature Switzerland AG 2025   127
J. Long, *Guide to Framing Design Practice for UX*, Synthesis Lectures
on Human-Centered Informatics, https://doi.org/10.1007/978-3-031-68981-9_11

Third, the many subordinate and superordinate relations between the initial UX description and the UX source material indicate that all three ways of increasing the overlap between the initial UX description and the UX source material would succeed.

11.1.2 Descriptors Additional to UX Initial Description

The rationale requires a criterion for the inclusion in the final UX description of descriptors not appearing in the initial UX description. The latter deriving from the UX source material contributions. Inclusion depends on their intended users. The larger and more varied the intended user group, the lower the criterion for inclusion.

The convention adopts the additional descriptors to the initial UX description be *Italicised* with initial letter in upper case. For example, *Website*. They are listed as for the source material contributions for easy access and editing. Given UX practitioners and UX researchers together constitute the largest and widest possible user group, the criterion selected is a single source material reference. This insures the most general application. However, a descriptor appearing in a particular UX practitioner contribution is counted only once, regardless of additional references in the same section. This is to avoid contribution source material bias.

The following points suggest themselves.

First, the number of the additional descriptors from the UX source material is large, compared with the overlap between the initial UX description and the UX source material.

Second, the range of the additional descriptors from the UX source material is extensive, compared with the overlap between the initial UX description and the UX source material.

Third, the number and range of the additional UX descriptors indicate that increasing their level of description would be one way of implementing the many subordinate and superordinate relations between the initial UX description and the UX source material.

11.1.3 Descriptors Retained From Initial UX Description

The rationale requires a criterion for the inclusion in the final UX description of descriptors appearing in the initial UX description. Inclusion depends on their intended users. The larger and more varied the intended user group, the lower the criterion for inclusion.

The convention adopts the retained descriptors from the initial UX description be in normal script and in lower case. Given UX practitioners and UX researchers together constitute the largest and widest possible user group, the criterion selected is a single reference. This insures the most general possible application.

Chapter Review

The chapter proposes a basis for the final UX description. It comprises—rationale and conventions, overlap between initial and final UX descriptions, descriptors additional to the initial UX description and descriptors retained from the initial UX description.

Chapter Carry Forward

The carry-forward from this chapter is shown in Appendix 2. It constitutes the basis for the final UX description and hence for the guide to framing design practice for UX. The appendix is intended to support readers in applying the final UX description to their own practice and to that of others. Also, in completing the associated exercise assignments. Appendix 2 is not for reading as a text in itself, but for consultation in its application.

11.2 Exercise Assignment

The exercise assignment is for all levels of UX design practitioning experience.

Consulting 11.1.1–11.1.3

– *Select* a UX practitioner group smaller than the total practitioner group selected here. For example, practitioners interested in best UX practice or practitioners interested primarily in UX business applications. Edit the final UX description to be appropriate for application by this smaller group.

Editing is most easily done on a digital version of the final UX description. However, editing can also be done on hard copy using different coloured highlight markers.

Consulting 11.1.1–11.1.3

– *Select* a UX researcher group smaller than the total researcher group selected here. For example, researchers interested in the effects of UX design, in the manner of, but not limited to, Experience-Centred Design (ECD) or researchers interested in real-time UX testing, in the manner of, but not limited to, funnel-testing. Edit the final UX description to be appropriate for this smaller group.

Editing is most easily done on a digital version of the final UX description. However, editing can also be done on hard copy using different coloured highlight markers.

Ways Forward for Framing UX Design Practice

12

12.1 Introduction

The book's guide frames current UX design practice. It comprises of the UX initial and final descriptions, the UX practitioner source material, the guide notes and the relations between them. However, it can also be used to propose new ways forward for framing UX design practice. All source materials agree that UX is alive and well with a bright future. However, there is little agreement on the conduct and reporting of such UX life and future. UX is currently practitioner-led and in a 'let a thousand flowers bloom' mode (Mao Zedong, Wikipedia). Thus, UX is strong on inclusivity but weak on exclusivity. In addition, it is strong on particularisation and weak on generalisation. For this reason, it is considered by the guide to be 'pre-formative'. There is only modest overlap between the source material and the initial UX description. More descriptors in common would indicate better agreement. The latter, then, is not a sound basis for proposing ways forward. An alternative is to use the same organisation as that of the guide itself. That is to say— UX, UX design practice, framing UX design practice, UX frameworks, UX approaches, UX methods and UX case studies.

12.2 Ways Forward for UX

The differences between UX source material contributions attest to many ways of thinking about UX and so of taking it forward. For example, Timmer considers that 'UX is a field, which has grown and fragmented.' The implication being that the field needs bringing together. He makes some specific proposals (4.6.1).

Further, Chakraborty considers that 'The growth in technology has become exponential and reshaped every aspect of our lives …and has become rather too complicated.' The

© The Author(s), under exclusive license to Springer Nature Switzerland AG 2025
J. Long, *Guide to Framing Design Practice for UX*, Synthesis Lectures
on Human-Centered Informatics, https://doi.org/10.1007/978-3-031-68981-9_12

implication being that UX should be less complicated in the sense of more coherent, for example, as in his Product-Centred Frame (4.4.2).

Last, Blyth urges UX practitioners 'to travel yet further, past UX as it is usually understood, and into new realms that have coloured differently again everything they were so confident of once before.' Such a way is framed by the concept of 'Muse'—a source of artistic inspiration, comprising of 'Art and delight, pragmatism and shipping, persuasion, dark patterns, tech-first innovation and AI (Artificial Intelligence) design'. The way forward for UX is to integrate the muses into its thinking, practice and research (4.7.1).

However, UX design practice needs to make good, as well as conceive, of such promise. Note that there is no contradiction between making UX less fragmented, more coherent and leaving current UX behind. To this extent, the way forward for UX could be common to the different ways implicated by the UX source materials.

12.3 Ways Forward for UX Design Practice

The differences between UX source material contributions attest to many ways of thinking about UX design practice and so of taking it forward. For example, Chakraborty considers that 'UX is tricky to define and problematic to own.' Further, that the 'UX designer's role (assuming there is such a role in a company) is often confined to designing a few widgets for the web page.' The implication being that companies need to 'own' UX and that its design practice needs to be appropriately implemented and properly valued (5.2.2).

Further, Cummaford considers, that HCI best-practice needs to be updated for UX. The implication being the application of his reformulation of best-practice for UX (5.3.1).

Last, Sinclair considers his laboratory-based usability studies to be central to UX design practice. The implication being that such studies are undervalued and need wider propagation (5.5.1–5.8).

However, UX design practice needs to make good, as well as conceive of, such promise. Note that the individual ways forward can be considered general, in as much as their conjoint conduct is not contradictory—for UX to be defined and owned, for UX best-practice to be updated and reformulated and for UX usability studies to be properly valued and more widely propagated.

12.4 Ways Forward for Framing UX Design Practice

The differences between UX source material contributions attest to many ways of thinking about framing UX design practice and so of taking it forward. For example, Blyth uses the novel concept of 'muse' to frame UX design practice—'Each (Muse)' has, since the turn of the century, presented the possibility that UX practice is neither necessary nor sufficient for 'quality' to exist. The implication being that UX practice needs to establish its own claims to designing 'quality' experiences (6.5.1).

Further, Chakraborty considers framing UX design practice 'acts as points of reference and an opportunity to simplify. They also perhaps help put in context the things that need to be thought about.' The implication being that UX design practice needs to review its scope, as in his Product-Centred design frame (6.4.1).

Last, framing UX design practice can be expressed as best-practice. Cummaford sets out the case—'Hardly surprising then, that commercial best-practice has attracted resources, resulting in its development and advancement.' The implication being that UX design practice needs to match, or at least take account of, such commercial best-practice (6.3.1).

However, framing UX design practice needs to make good, as well as conceive of, such promise. Note that the different ways can be carried forward together—using the concept of 'muse' to frame in a simplified and contextual manner, while taking account of commercial best-practice. Note that if more than a single framework is involved, for example 'muse' and 'product-centred', such joint carry-forward would require an additional superordinate framework to ensure compatibility.

12.5 Ways Forward for UX Frameworks

There are as many ways forward for UX frameworks as there are ways of framing. This is attested by the differences between UX source contributions. For example, Chakraborty considers that 'frameworks and frames act as points of reference and an opportunity to simplify. They also perhaps help put in context the things that need to be thought about.' The implication being that frameworks need 'definition, scope, and perceived utility'. His 'product-centric' framework proposes such a scope, comprising 'three intersecting circles, describing the cross-cutting concerns of business, technology and UX' (7.2.1).

Further, Middlemass considers that frameworks need to be comprehensive like his XD (Experience Design) framework. The latter comprises sections on XD Playbook, XD Practices, End2End Design, Development, Operations, Experience, Design Rules, Customer Experience and Business Analyst. The implication being that such comprehensiveness is rare in UX (7.4.1).

Last, Timmer proposes a 'design for performance framework' for UX, based on the conception of the cognitive engineering design problem (Dowell & Long, 1989). Emphasis is 'on the deficiency of performance, followed by respecification of the worksystem.' The latter including importantly a human 'cognitive' component.... Also, application of the concepts of 'desired' and 'actual' levels of performance, which assist in the framing of a 'design problem'. The implication being that UX frameworks need to support the design processes of diagnosis and prescription, absent from many UX frameworks (7.3.1).

All these ways forward show promise. However, for the promise to be made good as well as conceived, they need to be carried forward into the framing of UX design practice. The different ways can be carried forward together—all UX frameworks need to be defined, scoped and have perceived utility, to be comprehensive and to support performance. However, this generalisation is only at the highest level.

12.6 Ways Forward for UX Approaches

There are as many ways forward for UX approaches as there are ways of framing UX design practice. This is attested by the differences between UX source material contributions. For example, Sinclair applies a UX heuristics approach to review three flagship phones. The heuristics include efficiency, consistency, effort, flexibility, generalisation, clarity and feedback (8.4.5). The implication being that other UX practitioners, to be successful, would do well to follow his example. However, heuristics, as a feature, are essentially no more than 'rules of thumb' or 'hints and tips' for doing something. Here, they support a UX review or evaluation taking a UX approach. Although defined, they are not guaranteed to be optimal, guaranteed or rational (Long et al., 2023). However, they may be sufficient for reaching an immediate, short-term goal or approximation. Their validation in the longer term is still required.

Further, Timmer proposes a 'cognitive engineering' approach to UX. The latter includes web site analytics, AB testing and design specification (8.5.1). A key aspect of the engineering approach is the process of diagnosis, resulting in the specification of a design problem. This is expressed as the difference between desired and actual performance. The contrast is with the process of prescription, whereby the design process aligns desired and actual performance, such that the design problem is solved. This constitutes design for performance, typical of engineering approaches. The implication being that UX approaches are weak concerning both diagnosis and prescription.

Last, Grant uses a 'user-centred design (UCD) approach to the design of user experience.' The latter includes a 'steps' method, context of use, user requirements and design solutions (6.2.1). He concludes 'pleasurable (user) experience to be critical to both systems performance and personnel wellbeing. … a major control room project reported the changes improved the way users worked… made the environment more pleasurable. In contrast, frustration and discomfort are experiences to be avoided by design practice.'

All these ways forward show promise. However, for the promise to be made good, as well as conceived, they need to be carried forward into the framing of UX design practice. The different ways can be carried forward together and without contradiction are the need for validation, the inclusion of diagnosis and prescription and an emphasis on systems performance and personnel well-being.

12.7   Ways Forward for UX Methods

There are as many ways forward for UX methods as there are ways of framing UX design practice. This is attested by the differences between UX source material contributions. For example, Cummaford proposes a general best-practice methodology, including method as UX best-practice, changes to best-practice and mapping of best-practice and e-commerce systems (9.2.1).

Further, Grant uses a 'user-centred design' (UCD) steps method from BS EN ISO 9241-210. Understanding the context of use supports the following steps—specify the user requirements, produce design solutions and evaluate the design until a fit-for-purpose solution is found (9.3.1).

Last, Middlemass uses an XD method supported by a framework, including reporting lines, tools and notations, product, 'happy path' processes, best-practice and design needs (9.4.1–9.3).

All these ways forward show promise. However, for the promise to be made good as well as conceived, they need to be carried forward into the framing of UX design practice. There are essentially two types of design knowledge—declarative (substantive) is the 'what' of design and methodological is the 'how' of design. The latter presumes the former. There is little or no overlap between the methods referenced. In the absence of some actual or implied generality, the conjoint carry-forward of the individual methods remains problematic.

12.8   Ways Forward for UX Case Studies

Case studies are typically specified by the commissioning organisation and conducted by the UX practitioner, whether in-house or consultant. The specification may also include the nature and organisation of the report itself. Earlier such reports consisted mainly of text. The case study, reported by Sinclair, however, suggests a way forward for case study reporting (10.3.2).

This report includes images as well as text. In addition, the images and text are used to render the UX design and its progress more transparent. For example, by the use of 'heatmaps' to show the user journey. Heatmap 13.1 shows the Old Refrigeration Category Plan and Image 13.2 shows the New Refrigeration Category Plan (Figs. 12.1 and 12.2).

Sinclair has taken a leaf out of his own book here. 'And the most creative part of the user experience design process happens when you put users in front of a product. The friction between the product and the user is where novel solution(s) emerge....' Except in this case, the 'user' here is the reader of the case study report. The 'novel solutions' are the implementation of the report's recommendations.

This way forward for case study reporting could also be enhanced by importing the kind of material that usually appears on promotion sites. For example, in Sinclair's case

Fig. 12.1 Heatmap—old
refrigeration category plan

Fig. 12.2 Heatmap—new
refrigeration category plan

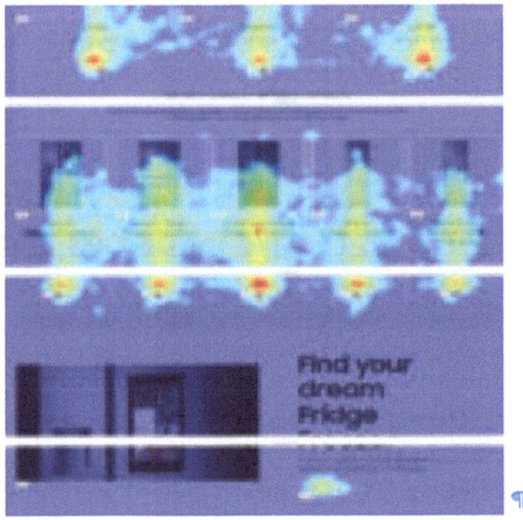

see http://paperst.co.uk/ux/case-studies/samsung-domestic-appliances-brilliant-basics/. A
fine line, however, has to be drawn between 'reporting' and 'promoting/advertising', but
that has always been the case.

Chapter Review

The guide is used as the basis for proposing ways forward for UX. Absence of agreement at this level of description between UX source material contributions means they cannot serve this purpose. However, individual different ways forward are not necessarily contradictory.

Chapter Carry Forward

The carry forward of ways forward proposed for UX is organised following the guide itself, that is—UX, UX design practice, framing UX design practice, UX frameworks, UX approaches, UX methods and UX case studies.

12.9 Exercise Assignment

The exercise assignment is intended to test readers' understanding and application of the concepts presented. Also to support tailoring the initial UX description to their own design requirements.

Consulting 12.2–12.7.

- *Check* the references cited for each way forward.
- *Identify* additional references from the source material (Chaps. 4–10), which strengthen the case for the particular way forward.
- *Identify* additional references from the source material (Chaps. 4–10), which weaken the case for the particular way forward.

Consulting the source material by chapter (4–10).

- *Suggest* additional ways forward for UX, as relate to each chapter.
- *Reflect* on the ease and difficulty of so doing.

References

Dowell, J., & Long, J. (1989). Towards a conception for an engineering discipline of human factors. *Ergonomics, 32*(11), 1513–1535.

Long, J., Cummaford, S., & Stork, A. (2023). *HCI design knowledge—Critique, challenge and a way forward*. Springer Nature.

Remaining Issues and Discussion 13

13.1 Introduction

In the previous chapter, the UX source material contributions are examined to propose ways forward for framing UX design practice. In so doing, a large and varied range of issues have been identified. However, in spite of this, there still remain issues for UX to address. These are now described. They are organised in the same way as both the guide and the previous chapter for easy access, comparison and checking. The issues comprise the following:

(1) UX

The different conceptions of UX need to be distinguished. These include—user experience, user design activity to achieve a desired user experience and a professional movement of practitioners. Some would also include understanding the effects of UX on social organisations (as in ECD or Experience-Centred Design).

(2) UX Design Practice

UX design practice needs to address implicit knowledge as concerns the acquisition and validation of UX design knowledge. This other than in terms of the UX practitioners' own increased design experience.

(3) Framing UX Design Practice

Framing UX design practice needs to specify its relations with HCI, in terms such as dominance, parity and subdominance or somesuch, rather than just 'usability.'

© The Author(s), under exclusive license to Springer Nature Switzerland AG 2025
J. Long, *Guide to Framing Design Practice for UX*, Synthesis Lectures
on Human-Centered Informatics, https://doi.org/10.1007/978-3-031-68981-9_13

(4) UX Frameworks

UX frameworks need to address the validation of design knowledge in terms such as conceptualisation, operationalisation, test and generalisation or somesuch.

(5) UX Approaches

UX approaches need to address both implicit and explicit design knowledge. In particular, how explicit UX design knowledge, comprising declarative 'what' knowledge, can support implicit UX design practitioner design experience in the application of UX methods.

(6) Methods

UX methods need to address how explicit UX design knowledge can support implicit UX practitioner design experience.

(7) UX Case Studies

UX case studies need to address how to generalise over projects and the associated case studies.

13.2   Remaining Issues

These issues are now addressed in detail.

13.2.1 Remaining Issues for UX

UX means 'user experience'. However, it is used in more than one sense in the UX practitioner source contributions. This leads to a lack of clarity at least and a lack of understanding at worst.

First, as expressed in the initial UX description 'conscious events/knowledge and skills', UX refers to the user. And in particular, to the user's experience, for example, pleasure, well-being, frustration, impatience and so on. The frustration experience results, for example, from the user's interaction with a poorly designed business website to purchase a product.

Second, as expressed by the UX descriptor 'design practice', it refers to the activities of the designer. That is, to their design practice, for example specification and implementation of an e-commerce website to increase the user's engagement to purchase a product, such as a domestic appliance. The associated experience should be pleasurable and not frustrating.

Last, as expressed by the descriptor UX 'movement', it can also denote the UX community/field of study.

Of course, the three meanings are related, in that the UX designer, who belongs to the UX movement, designs a UX experience for the user, who internalises the experience. For example, the UX-skilled specification and implementation of an e-information website to increase the user's engagement to sign up for a subscription.

However, the meanings are importantly different. They are sometimes disambiguated by their context, but this is the exception. Readers unpersuaded by this argument might consider the following quotes selected from the source material contributions. Associated questions and comments are in brackets.

'Many of those same practitioners now believe in the precepts of UX, as fervently as they did usability'. (Are the UX precepts of experience, of UX design or of both?)

'The topic of UX is complex and struggles with definition, scope and perceived utility.' (Do definition, scope and perceived utility apply to user experience, to UX design or to both?)

'Future research needs to take account of how to apply current best-practice as part of a UX approach.' (Does approach refer to user experience, to UX design or to both?)

'While UX has become essential, it inhabits an uncomfortable space, where it's tricky to define and problematic to own. The UX designer's role....' (This quote is included as a possible example of disambiguation.)

UX needs to distinguish explicitly these different meanings and their relations. For example, UXuser (or UXu) might be used to refer to the user experience or alternatively UXexperience (or UXe). UXdesigner (or UXd) might be used to refer to the designer's practice to engender that experience or alternatively UX design practice (or UXdp). UXmovement (or UXm) might be used to denote the UX movement or alternatively UXcommunity (or UXc). Undifferentiated UX might be used to refer to all three meanings, but this would need to be made clear by the context. Although differentiation sounds complicated, once the particular meaning has been made clear, context could be made to do the rest.

As a final comment concerning UX experience, the paucity of types of experience instanced by the UX source material contributions is a long way from Wikipedia's six categories of experience, as physical, mental, emotional, spiritual, social and virtual. And even further from the 47 types of experiences also identified. These include experiences such as aesthetics, as in beauty, conflict, as in destructive relations, friendship, as in ties to others mortality, as in death and self-fulfilment, as in pride of self (1.1.2). There is no mention of any of these experiences in the UX source materials.

13.2.2 Remaining Issues for UX Design Practice

UX design practice research acquires and validates UX design knowledge to support UX design practice. Since much UX practitioner's design knowledge is implicit, UX design practice research needs to acquire and to validate implicit as well as explicit such knowledge. The former includes the ideas that UX practitioners are working together to advance. Further, it might relate to recent designs of other UX designers, which have made an impression on the practitioner and which they want to try out themselves. The UX source material contributions, however, makes little or no reference to UX design practice research:

'I love the simplicity of the idea at its (UX) core—Test and Iterate.' (No reference to specification, so not much room for research, then?)

'The growth in technology has become exponential and reshaped every aspect of our lives. From mobility to metaverse, Internet of things to augmented reality, the world of experience'. (No mention of research making a contribution to this exponential growth in technology.)

'Another common path for UX practitioners, in the last twenty years, has been to move from UX research to UX design and then into product management.' (This suggests a reduction in UX research.)

'Key insights are captured from research *Standards, Guidance* etc.' (This is included as an exception, which comes from a UCD practitioner, eschewing the term UX.)

Further, with no mention of UX design practice research, there can be no address of the acquisition and validation of UX implicit design knowledge, other than in terms of the UX practitioners' own increased design experience. It is worth noting that academic UX research is not of much help here (with or without the ubiquitous lens). What research there is looks more like UX practice than UX research. For example the exploration of new technology (under the guise of 'having a look at it'). Also, the design of novel applications, but with no associated test of frameworks, approaches or methods etc. It is unclear how this type of research supports researchers building on each other's work and so making progress in the acquisition and validation of UX design knowledge. An example follows. It has been anonymised for obvious reasons.

'Abstract: This talk will introduce X Motion, a suite of software applications developed since Summer 2020, by over 150 students and academics at X's Department of X. The software enables a variety of pathways of touchless interactions with a computer using a standard webcam and laptop running X. It enables touchless capability for the majority of existing X applications without further modifications and encompasses several AI and Computer Vision models from leading organisations. User interactions are facilitated as mixed modalities such as combinations of speech commands, in-air touchpoints simulation, digital ink simulation, finger and hand recognition gestures, 2D-3D depth approximation, facial navigation, facial switches and whole-body movements including shaped gesture patterns. It has been optimised for latency and suitability in a variety of touchless computing use cases in collaboration with X partners at X, X and X, developed as an alternative input for a keyboard, mouse, or joypad. This includes for gaming, population health, accessibility and digital healthcare. This talk will cover a brief overview on each of these, followed by a focused discussion into clinical applications for this technology. The urgency and importance of this development was significant during the COVID-19 pandemic period, when the NHS needed more hygienic ways to interact with shared computers and new ways to consult with their patients from afar'.

13.2.3 Remaining Issues for Framing UX Design Practice

HCI is the 'elephant in the room', when it comes to general discussions of UX. It is occasionally mentioned in the UX source material, but the relationship is not addressed in any detail. When UX is contrasted historically with preceding design activities, it is usually only in terms of 'usability'. This is the more surprising, since the UX contributions recognise usability as being a prime determinant of a 'good' user experience. So, what is the relationship between UX and HCI?

The UX source material generally associates UX with experience and HCI with usability. However, this does not take us very far. There are UX source contributions, which espouse usability, for example, as an aspect of the customer journey (8.4.4). In contrast, there are HCI source contributions, which espouse experience in the form of feelings, as an aspect of UCD performance (5.4.1).

There are three main types of relation, which might hold for framing UX design practice. They are dominant, parity and subdominant. Each is discussed in turn.

1. Dominant denotes a relationship in which UX is conceived as primary and so superordinate with respect to HCI. In this case, the latter would be understood to articulate the HCI experience of the customer journey, for example, primarily in terms of usability. Source material contributions provide evidence of such a relationship (8.4.4). HCI would then become just one aspect or one way of doing UX.
2. Parity denotes a relationship in which UX and HCI are conceived as equal or functionally identical. They would both address any and all issues related to users interacting with computers to do something as desired. The model here could be something like Human Factors and Ergonomics. Historically, the former was concerned primarily with mental tasks and originated in the US. The latter was concerned mainly with physical tasks and originated in the UK. The two terms are now synonymous both in the US and the UK. However, primary historical usage still prevails in some contexts. Alternatively, HCI and UX might be considered subordinate to the general field of computer technology, although it is unclear whether the latter is intended to denote computer science.

3. Subdominant denotes a relationship in which UX is conceived as secondary and so subordinate to HCI. In this case, the latter would be understood to articulate the UX experience of the customer's usability journey, for example, in terms of feelings, such as frustration and well-being in the workplace. Source material contributions provide evidence of such a relationship (4.3.3). UX would become just one aspect or one way of doing HCI. This relationship would be much like those of innovation, art, craft, applied psychology, science and engineering with respect to HCI, as described by Long (2021). In addition, subdominant UX might end up as being no more than 'HCI for websites'. The source material contributions make little or no reference to other domains of application. The one exception is safety critical environments, such as defence, nuclear and rail (4.3.4). The source contributor, however, considers themselves to be a UCD practitioner and does not use the term UX to refer to their own design practice.

13.2.4 Remaining Issues for UX Frameworks

Validation of knowledge comprises four superordinate concepts—conceptualisation, operationalisation, test and generalisation (Long, 2021). Conceptualisation expresses knowledge as concepts and their relations. Operationalisation makes the concepts and their relations observable and hence recordable and measurable. Test assesses the operationalised concepts and relations. Generalisation cumulates the successfully tested operationalised concepts. Validation applies the criteria of completeness, coherence and fitness-for-purpose to superordinate concepts. The UX source material contributions make no reference to validation in these terms or even in any very clear equivalent terms. Neither do they mention how practitioners' might validate their own implicit design knowledge. Validation is not addressed.

'One useful way to re-frame is the 'product-centric framing', which positions three intersecting circles, describing the cross-cutting concerns of business, technology and UX (7.2.1)'. (This is an initial proposal, so pre-validatory. However, the future need for validation and their associated difficulties is not mentioned.)

The XD Playbook framework structure is explicit and detailed. The relations between elements are identified. Notes provide additional clarification (7.4.1). (Although pre-validatory, the framework shows promise for validation. However, it is not mentioned. Further, the design practice context suggests it to be unlikely.)

13.2.5 Remaining Issues for UX Approaches

Approach implies scope, structure and perspective. Scope delimits an approach. Its structure is that to which parts are added. Its perspective is a general way of viewing UX. The latter embodies all these descriptors. The remaining issue, however, is that the descriptors may be implicit or explicit in the denotation of a UX practitioner's framing of design practice for UX. This critical distinction, however, is not recognised by the UX source material.

'Follow the processes, place users at the heart of each step, measure for effectiveness, efficiency and satisfaction, and a good result will follow' (10.3.1).

'Future research needs to take account of how to apply current best-practice (as listed) as part of a UX approach' (5.3.1). (The listing here is explicit. There is no mention of implicit 'best-practice'.)

'In a nutshell, Samsung scores relatively poorly on the marketing journey. It scores low on effort, generalisation and clarity' (10.2). (The scoring criteria are all explicit. It is unclear how implicit criteria could be scored.)

'To compliment multiple design changes to pages, it is possible to conduct 'split' testing, or AB Testing' (8.5.2). (AB testing is specified and implemented and so, explicit. Implicit AB testing is not plausible.)

Approaches, then, need to accommodate implicit as well as explicit descriptors of framing design practice for UX.

13.2.6 Remaining Issues for UX Methods

Method denotes a procedure, a process or a technique for attaining a goal or purpose. These means are supported by methodological or 'how' knowledge. The contrast is with declarative, substantive or 'what' knowledge. The degree of support, provided by methodological knowledge, depends on its effectiveness. That is the confidence it affords the successful attainment of a goal. The two main types of method are 'implement and test' and 'specify and implement'.

'Implement and test' is a natural method for UX. It fits well with the design experience of the practitioner.

'I'm lucky that I do UX. I love the simplicity of the idea at its core—test and iterate' (4.2.1). ('Test and iterate' is assumed to equate with 'implement and test', as a method and both to equate with 'trial and error'.)

'Specify and implement', however, is a less natural method for UX. In much design practice, specification is explicit, recruiting declarative (substantive) or 'what' knowledge to support design. This may be in the form of standards, guidelines, principles, precepts, best-practice or theories. If UX practitioners simply apply the latter according to their own design experience, it is unclear that, and how, the effectiveness of the 'what' knowledge is assured. Without such assurance, what confidence is afforded the successful engagement of a design goal?

'Artefact specification', as a feature, describes what the to-be-designed 'artefact is like'. 'Artefact 1, for example, is 'As-Is'. 'Artefact 2, for example is the user's journey'. Specification, as proposed here, is detailed and explicit' (7.4.2).

Both methods are able to accommodate implicit and explicit UX design knowledge, as embodied in the personal experience of the UX designer. Always assuming that a UX practitioner's 'very idea' of a new application counts as a specification. Both methods are also able to accommodate explicit design knowledge, acquired by UX research only 'specify and implement' is able to recruit explicit UX design knowledge to a method (explicitly).

The remaining issue for UX, then, is how explicit UX design knowledge, comprising declarative 'what' knowledge, can support implicit UX design practitioner personal experience in the application of UX methods.

13.2.7 Remaining Issues for UX Case Studies

The case studies reported or referenced by the UX practitioners' source material are all single case studies, typically of an individual project. Fine as far as it goes. But case studies are also required to generalise over projects and the associated case studies for wider application.

Following Long (2021), generalisation of knowledge requires the cumulating of successfully tested operationalised concepts, including their relations. Criteria include completeness, coherence and fitness-for-purpose No such generalisations appear in the UX source material.

'The case study report is of a project. It reviews three flagship phones and describes the phone accessories marketing and upsell journeys' (10.2). (The review uses heuristics to conduct the case study. There is no attempt to test or develop the heuristics further as might be required for generalisation.)

'The project attempted to improve the user experience of buying domestic appliances from a major supplier. This entailed reconciling two different sitemaps. A lab-based usability study was conducted and reported as a case study' (10.3.1). (There was no attempt to identify, to test or to develop the method used in the study as might be required for generalisation).

Chapter Review

This chapter addresses issues remaining, as concern the framing of UX design practice. The issues are in addition to those raised by the ways forward, identified by the previous chapter. UX and user experience are distinguished. A way for UX design practice to address implicit design knowledge is proposed. How UX design practice might relate to HCI is proposed. A way for UX frameworks to address validation is described. How UX approaches might address both implicit and explicit design knowledge is presented. Also suggested is how

UX methods' address of explicit UX design knowledge might support implicit UX design practitioner personal experience. Last, a way to generalise UX case studies is suggested.

13.3 Exercise Assignment

The exercise assignment is intended to test readers' understanding and application of the concepts presented. Also to support tailoring the initial UX description to their own design requirements.

Consulting 13.2–13.7 and for each section:

– *Identify* additional remaining issues not raised in the section or in the previous chapter.
– *Reference* these additional issues with the academic or professional literature.
– *Note* any failures to reference.
– *Why* might this be so?

Reference

Long, J. (2021) *Approaches and frameworks for HCI research.* Cambridge University Press.

Appendix 1—Carry Forward of the Initial Description for Framing UX Design Practice from Chaps. 1–3

Abstract

The carry-forward from Chaps. 1–3 is presented. It constitutes the basis for the initial UX description and hence for the guide to framing design practice for UX. The appendix is intended to support readers in applying the initial UX description to the UX practitioner source material, presented in Chaps. 4–10. Also, in completing the associated exercise assignments. Appendix 1 is not for reading as a text in itself, but for consulting to make its application easier.

1. Chapter 1 Initial Description for UX

The numbers preceding the section shows the chapter and the section. For example, 1.1 indicates Chap. 1, Sect. 1. The number following the section shows the original chapter and section number, for example, 'UX User (1.1.2)'. Carry Forward and Descriptors are both listed.

1.1 UX User (1.1.2)

Carry-forward—'a User is Someone, who uses Human–Computer Technology To Do Something (Act) as Intended (Intention)'.

Descriptors
   User/Someone/Human–Computer Technology/Act/Intention.

J. Long, *Guide to Framing Design Practice for UX*, Synthesis Lectures on Human-Centered Informatics, https://doi.org/10.1007/978-3-031-68981-9

1.2 UX Experience (1.2.2)

Carry Forward—'Conscious Events and the Knowledge and Skills derived from them'.

Descriptors

- Conscious Events/Knowledge and Skills.

1.3 UX User Experience (1.3.2)

Carry-forward—'Conscious Events and the Knowledge and Skills derived from them, which result in a User Experience for Someone, who uses Human–Computer Technology To Do Something (Act), as Intended (Intention)'.

Descriptors

- Conscious Events/Knowledge and Skills/User Experience/Someone/Human–Computer Technology/Act/Intention.

1.4 UX Movement (1.4.2)

Carry-forward—'Professional Change and Development of a Group of People Working Together to Advance their Shared Ideas.'

Descriptors

- Professional Change and Development/Group of People/Working Together/Advance/Shared Ideas.

1.5 UX Problem (1.5.2)

Carry-forward—'User Experience Problem, and User Experience Solution, which describe the Shared User Experience Ideas, which Practitioners are working together to Advance'.

Descriptors

- User Experience Problem/User Experience Solution/Shared User Experience Ideas/Working Together/Practitioner/Advance.

1.6 UX General Problem (1.6.2)

Carry-forward—'User Experience General Problems associated with User experience General Solutions, which describe the Shared Ideas, which Practitioners are Working Together to Advance'.

Descriptors

- User Experience General Problems/User Experience General Solutions/Shared Ideas/ Practitioners/Working Together/Advance.

1.7 UX General Design Problem (1.7.2)

Carry Forward—'UX General Design Problem is to Specify and to Implement Human–Computer Technology for a User as Someone, who uses Human–Computer Technology to do Something (Act), as Intended (Intention), which results in experience comprising conscious events and the knowledge and skills derived from them.'

Descriptors

- UX General Design Problem/Specify/Implement/Human–Computer Technology/Act/ Intention.

1.8 UX Particular Scope (1.8.2)

Carry-forward—'UX Design Problem and UX Design Solution to Specify and to Implement Human–Computer Technology for Users as People, who use Human–Computer Technology to Do Something (Act) as Intended (Intention), which results in an Experience comprising Conscious Events and the Knowledge and Skills derived from them'.

Descriptors

- UX Design Problem/UX Design Solution/Specify/Implement Human–Computer Technology/Users/People/Act/Intention/Experience/Conscious Events/Knowledge and Skills.

1.9 State of UX General Design Problem and UX General Design Problem Particular Scope (1.9)

Carry-forward—'UX General Design Problem and UX General Design Problem Particular Scope to Specify and to Implement Human–Computer Technology for User Experience'.

Descriptors

- UX General Design Problem/UX General Design Problem Particular Scope/Specify/ Implement/Human–Computer Technology/User Experience.

1.10 Critique and Challenge for UX General Design Problem and UX General Design Problem Particular Scope (1.10)

Carry-forward—'User Experience General Design Problem and User Experience General Design Problem Particular Scope to Specify and to Implement Human–Computer Technology for User Experience'.

Descriptors

- UX General Design Problem/UX General Design Problem Particular Scope/Specify/ Implement/Human–Computer Technology/User Experience.

1.11 UX Research (1.11)

Carry-Forward—'Acquisition and Validation of Implicit UX Knowledge and Explicit UX Knowledge to support UX Design Practice.'

Descriptors

- Acquisition/Validation/Implicit UX Knowledge/Explicit UX Knowledge/UX Design Practice.

2. Chapter 2 Initial Description for UX Design Practice

2.1 Design General (2.1.1)

Carry Forward—'Design Representation'.

Descriptors

– Design Representation.

2.2 UX Design (2.1.2)

Carry-forward—'UX Design Representation'.

Descriptors

– UX Design Representation.

2.3 Practice General (2.2.1)

Carry-forward—'Practice and Performance'.

Descriptors

– Practice/Performance.

2.4 UX Practice (2.2.2)

Carry Forward—'UX Practice and UX Performance.'
    Descriptors/UX Practice/UX Performance.

2.5 Design Practice General (2.3.1)

Carry-forward—'Specify Representations and Design Performance, as Implement Representations.'

Descriptors

– Specify Representations/Design Performance/Implement Representations.

2.6 UX Design Practice (2.3.2)

Carry-forward—'Specify UX Representations and UX Performance as Implement UX Representations.'

Descriptors

– Specify UX Representations/UX Performance/Implement UX Representations.

2.7 State of UX Design Practice (2.4)

Carry-forward—'Specify UX Representations and UX Design Performance as Implement UX Representations'.

Descriptors

– Specify UX Representations/UX Design Performance/Implement UX Representations.

2.8 UX Critique and Challenge for UX Design Practice (2.5)

Carry-forward—'Specify UX Representations and UX Design Performance, as Implement UX Representations'.

Descriptors

– Specify UX Representations/UX Design Performance/Implement UX Representations.

2.9 UX Design Practice Research (2.6)

Carry Forward—'Acquisition and Validation of Implicit UX Knowledge and Explicit UX Knowledge to support UX Design Practice'.

Descriptors

– Acquisition/Validation/Implicit UX Knowledge/Explicit UX Knowledge/UX Design Practice.

3. Chapter 3 Initial Description for Framing Ux Design Practice

3.1 Framing General (3.1.1)

Carry-forward—'Framing, as Application of Structures'.

Descriptors

– Framing/Application/Structures.

3.2 Framing UX (3.1.2)

Framework (3.1.2.1)

Carry-forward—'Framework, as Application of Structures for Frame and Framing'.

Descriptors

– Framework/Application/Structures/Frame/Framing.

3.3 Approach (3.1.2.2)

Carry-forward—'Approach, as Application of Structures having Scope, Structure and Perspective'.

Descriptors

– Approach/Application/Structures/Scope/Structure/Perspective.

3.4 Method (3.1.2.3)

Carry-forward—'Method, as Application of Method Structure Types'.

Descriptors

– Method/Application/Structure/Types.

3.5 Implement and Test (3.1.2.3.1)

Carry-forward—'Application of Structures of Implement and Test'.

Descriptors

– Application/Structures/Implement/Test.

3.6 Specify and Implement (3.1.2.3.2)

Carry forward—'Application of Structures of Specify and Implement'.

Descriptors

– Application/Structures/Specify/Implement.

3.7 Specify then Implement (3.1.2.3.3)

Carry-forward—'Application of Structures of Specify then Implement'.

Descriptors Retained

– Application/Structures/Specify/Implement.

3.8 Case Study (3.1.2.4)

Carry-forward—'Application of Structures as in Organising and Reporting a Case Study'.

Descriptors

– Application/Structures/Organising/Reporting/Case Study Report.

3.9 Framing Design General (3.2.1)

Carry Forward—'Design Representation'.

Descriptors

– Design Representation.

3.10 Framing UX Design (3.2.2)

Carry Forward = 'UX Design Representation'.

Descriptors
   UX Design Representation.

3.11 Framing Practice General (3.3.1)

Carry Forward—Practice as Performance.

Descriptors

Practice/Performance.

3.12 Framing UX Practice (3.3.2)

Carry-forward—'Application of Structures of UX Framework, of UX Approach, of UX Method and of UX Case Study'.

Descriptors

– Application/Structures/UX Framework/UX Approach/UX Method/UX Case Study.

3.13 Framing Design Practice General (3.4.1)

Carry-forward—'Specify Representations and Implement Representations'.

Descriptors

– Specify/Representation/Implement/Representation.

3.14 Framing UX Design Practice (3.4.2)

Carry Forward—'Specify Representations and Implement Representations'.

Descriptors

– Specify Representations/Implement Representations.

3.15 State of Framing UX Design Practice (3.5)

Carry-forward—Specify UX Representations and UX Design Performance as Implement UX Representations'.

Descriptors

– Specify UX Representations/UX Design Performance/Implement UX Representations.

3.16 Critique and Challenge for Framing UX Design Practice (3.6)

Carry Forward—Specify UX Representations and UX Design Performance as Implement UX Representations'.

Descriptors

– Specify UX Representations/UX Design Performance/Implement UX Representations.

3.17 Framing UX Design Practice Research (3.7)

Carry Forward—UX Conduct and UX Reporting.

Descriptors

– UX Conduct/UX Reporting.

Appendix 1 Review

The appendix presents an initial UX description. The latter is expressed in terms of everyday language. It comprises—UX, UX design practice and framing UX design practice. The listing of the descriptors is to support readers in applying the description to the UX practitioner source material, presented in Chaps. 4–10 and in completing the exercise assignments.

Appendix 2—Carry-Forward of the Final Description for Framing UX Design Practice from Chap. 11

Abstract

The carry-forward from Chap. 11 is presented. Initial UX descriptors used by the UX source material contributions are shown in **Bold**, with the initial letter in upper case, for example **User** and **Human–Computer Technology**. They are also listed at the end in alphabet order. Additional descriptors to the initial UX description are *Italicised* with initial letter in upper case, for example, *Website* and *Human–Computer Interaction*. They are listed as for the source material contributions, but for easy access and editing. The list is in alphabet order. Together they constitute the basis for the final UX description and hence for the guide to framing design practice for UX. The appendix is intended to support UX practitioners and UX researchers in applying the final UX description to their own practices. Also, to support readers in completing the associated exercise assignments. Appendix 2 is not for reading as a text in itself, but for consulting to make its application easier.

2.1 UX User (1.1.2)

Carry-forward—'a User is Someone, who uses Human–Computer Technology To Do Something (Act) as Intended (Intention)'.

Descriptors

User/Someone/Human–Computer Technology/Act/Intention.

2.2 UX Experience (1.2.2)

Carry Forward—'Conscious Events and the Knowledge and Skills derived from them'.

J. Long, *Guide to Framing Design Practice for UX*, Synthesis Lectures on Human-Centered Informatics, https://doi.org/10.1007/978-3-031-68981-9

Descriptors

– Conscious Events/Knowledge and Skills.

2.3 UX User Experience (1.3.2)

Carry-forward—'Conscious Events and the Knowledge and Skills derived from them, which result in a User Experience for Someone, who uses Human–Computer Technology To Do Something (Act), as Intended (Intention)'.

Descriptors

– Conscious Events/Knowledge and Skills/**User Experience**/Someone/Human–Computer Technology/Act/Intention.

2.4 UX Movement (1.4.2)

Carry-forward—'Professional Change and Development of a Group of People Working Together to Advance their Shared Ideas.'

Descriptors

– **Professional Change and Development**/Group of People/Working Together/Advance/ Shared Ideas.

2.5 UX Problem (1.5.2)

Carry-forward—'User Experience Problem, and User Experience Solution, which describe the Shared User Experience Ideas, which Practitioners are working together to Advance'.

Descriptors

– User Experience Problem/User Experience Solution/Shared User Experience Ideas/ Working Together/**Practitioner**/Advance.

2.6 UX General Problem (1.6.2)

Carry-forward—'User Experience General Problems associated with User experience General Solutions, which describe the Shared Ideas, which Practitioners are Working Together to Advance'.

Descriptors

– User Experience General Problems/User Experience General Solutions/Shared Ideas/ Practitioners/Working Together/Advance.

2.7 UX General Design Problem (1.7.2)

Carry Forward—'UX General Design Problem is to Specify and to Implement Human– Computer Technology for a User as Someone, who uses Human–Computer Technology to do Something (Act), as Intended (Intention), which results in experience comprising conscious events and the knowledge and skills derived from them.'

Descriptors

– UX General Design Problem/Specify/Implement/Human–Computer Technology/Act/ Intention.

2.8 UX Particular Scope (1.8.2)

Carry-forward—'UX Design Problem and UX Design Solution to Specify and to Implement Human–Computer Technology for Users as People, who use Human–Computer Technology to Do Something (Act) as Intended (Intention), which results in an Experience comprising Conscious Events and the Knowledge and Skills derived from them'.

Descriptors

– UX Design Problem/UX Design Solution/Specify/Implement Human–Computer Technology/Users/People/Act/Intention/Experience/Conscious Events/Knowledge and Skills.

2.9 State of UX General Design Problem and UX General Design Problem Particular Scope (1.9)

Carry-forward—'UX General Design Problem and UX General Design Problem Particular Scope to Specify and to Implement Human–Computer Technology for User Experience'.

Descriptors

- UX General Design Problem/UX General Design Problem Particular Scope/Specify/Implement/Human–Computer Technology/User Experience.

2.10 Critique and Challenge for UX General Design Problem and UX General Design Problem Particular Scope (1.10)

Carry-forward—'User Experience General Design Problem and User Experience General Design Problem Particular Scope to Specify and to Implement Human–Computer Technology for User Experience'.

Descriptors

- UX General Design Problem/UX General Design Problem Particular Scope/Specify/Implement/Human–Computer Technology/User Experience.

2.11 UX Research (1.11)

Carry-Forward—'Acquisition and Validation of Implicit UX Knowledge and Explicit UX Knowledge to support UX Design Practice.'

Descriptors

- Acquisition/Validation/Implicit UX Knowledge/Explicit UX Knowledge/UX Design Practice.

2.12 Design General (2.1.1)

Carry Forward—'Design Representation'.

Descriptors

– Design Representation/*Feedback* (subordinate to *Design* and *User-Centred Design* (*UCD*)).

2.13 UX Design (2.1.2)

Carry-forward—'UX Design Representation'.

Descriptors

– UX Design Representation.

2.14 Practice General (2.2.1)

Carry-forward—'Practice and Performance'.

Descriptors

– Practice/Performance.

2.15 UX Practice (2.2.2)

Carry Forward—'UX Practice and UX Performance.'

Descriptors

– UX Practice/UX Best-Practice (subordinate to UX Practice and superordinate to Funnel Testing)/UX Practice (superordinate to Funnel Testing)/Online AB Testing (subordinate to UX Practice/Prototype and Requirements/Usability and subordinate to UX Practice/Tools).

2.16 Design Practice General (2.3.1)

Carry-forward—'Specify Representations and Design Performance, as Implement Representations.'

Descriptors

– Specify Representations/Design Performance/Implement Representations.

2.17 UX Design Practice (2.3.2)

Carry-forward—'Specify UX Representations and UX Performance as Implement UX Representations.'

Descriptors

– Specify UX Representations/UX Performance/Implement UX Representations:

2.18 State of UX Design Practice (2.4)

Carry-forward—'Specify UX Representations and UX Design Performance as Implement UX Representations'.

Descriptors

– Specify UX Representations/UX Design Performance/Implement UX Representations.

2.19 UX Critique and Challenge for Ux Design Practice (2.5)

Carry-forward—'Specify UX Representations and UX Design Performance, as Implement UX Representations'.

Descriptors

– Specify UX Representations/UX Design Performance/Implement UX Representations.

2.20 UX Design Practice Research (2.6)

Carry Forward—'Acquisition and Validation of Implicit UX Knowledge and Explicit UX Knowledge to support UX Design Practice'.

Descriptors

– Acquisition/Validation/Implicit UX Knowledge/Explicit UX Knowledge/UX Design Practice.

2.21 Framing General (3.1.1)

Carry-forward—'Framing, as Application of Structures'.

Descriptors

– Framing/Application/Structures.

2.22 Framing UX (3.1.2)

2.23 Framework (3.1.2.1)

Carry-forward—'Framework, as Application of Structures for Frame and Framing'.

Descriptors

– **Framework**/Application/Structures/**Frame**/Framing.

2.24 Approach (3.1.2.2)

Carry-forward—'Approach, as Application of Structures having Scope, Structure and Perspective'.

Descriptors

– **Approach**/Application/Structures/Scope/Structure/Perspective.

2.25 Method (3.1.2.3)

Carry-forward—'Method, as Application of Method Structure Types'.

Descriptors

– **Method**/Application/Structure/Types.

2.26 Implement and Test (3.1.2.3.1)

Carry-forward—'Application of Structures of Implement and Test'.

Descriptors

– Application/Structures/Implement/Test.

2.27 Specify and Implement (3.1.2.3.2)

Carry forward—'Application of Structures of Specify and Implement'.

Descriptors

– Application/Structures/Specify/Implement.

2.28 Specify then Implement (3.1.2.3.3)

Carry-forward—'Application of Structures of Specify then Implement'.

Descriptors Retained

– Application/Structures/Specify/Implement.

2.29 Case Study (3.1.2.4)

Carry-forward—'Application of Structures as in Organising and Reporting a Case Study'.

Descriptors

– Application/Structures/Organising/Reporting/**Case Study**.

2.30 Framing Design General (3.2.1)

Carry Forward—'Design Representation'.

Descriptors

– Design Representation.

2.31 Framing UX Design (3.2.2)

Carry Forward = 'UX Design Representation'.

Descriptors

UX Design Representation.

2.32 Framing Practice General (3.3.1)

Carry Forward—Practice as Performance.

Descriptors

Practice/Performance.

2.33 Framing UX Practice (3.3.2)

Carry-forward—'Application of Structures of UX Framework, of UX Approach, of UX Method and of UX Case Study'.

Descriptors

– Application/Structures/UX Framework/UX Approach/UX Method/UX Case Study.

2.34 Framing Design Practice General (3.4.1)

Carry-forward—'Specify Representations and Implement Representations'.

Descriptors

– Specify/Representation/Implement/Representation.

2.35 Framing UX Design Practice (3.4.2)

Carry Forward—'Specify Representations and Implement Representations'.

Descriptors

– Specify Representations/Implement Representations.

2.36 State of Framing UX Design Practice (3.5)

Carry-forward—Specify UX Representations and UX Design Performance as Implement UX Representations'.

Descriptors

– Specify UX Representations/UX Design Performance/Implement UX Representations.

2.37 Critique and Challenge for Framing UX Design Practice (3.6)

Carry Forward—Specify UX Representations and UX Design Performance as Implement UX Representations'.

Descriptors

– Specify UX Representations/UX Design Performance/Implement UX Representations.

2.38 Framing UX Design Practice Research (3.7)

Carry Forward—UX Conduct and UX Reporting.

Descriptors

– UX Conduct/UX Reporting.

List of Initial UX Descriptors Used by the UX Source Material

Approach/Case   Study/Frame/Framework/Method/User/User   Experience/ Performance/Practice/Practitioner/Professional Change and Development
Descriptors Additional to the Initial UX Description Derived from the UX Source Material

UX in General

Assets/Banner   Advert/Best-Practice/Business/Channel/Client/Trust/Consumer/Customer/ Definition/Digital/Marketing/Discomfort/Engagement/Environment/Era   of   Exponential/Field/Financial   Expenses/Frustration/HCI/HCI   with   Ergonomics/HumanFactors/ Marketing/PerceivedUtility/Pleasure/Practitioners/Product-Centric/Frame/Purchasing/ Journey/Sales/Sitemap/Stakeholders/Test-And-Iterate/Topic of UX/UCD/User Journey/UX Design/UXHXCX/Virtual Assistant/Work.

UX Design Practice

Accept Terms and Conditions/Analytics Data/Approaches/Atomic Design Methods/ Augmented Reality/Best-Practice/Business/Buttons/Buy Now-Call to Action/Checkout/ Commonplace Book/Confirmation Page/Consumers/Conversion/Funnel/Conversion Rate/ Customers/Customers/3D Virtual Space/Design Methods/Desktop/Digital Channel/ Equipment/Ergonomics//Feedback/Financial Details/Guidance/Human Factors/Lean UX Design Methods/LinearDevelopmenCycle/Metaverse/Internet of Things/Minimum Viable Product (MVP)/Mobile/Mobility/Online AB Testing/Online Funnel Testing/Online Scaled Up User Testing/Online Transaction Testing/Pages/Personal Details/Practice/ Product Category Detail Page/Product Detail Page/Projects/Usability Study/Prototype/ Prototype Testing/Quote and Buy Service/Quote Page/Buy Now/Sample Search Landing Page/Sessions/Tree Test/Sitemap/Standards/Subjective User Data/Tablet/Technology/ Transaction Process/Tried-and-Tested Methods/UCD/UseErrors/User Journey/Tag/Virtual Life/Visitors/Walk Through//Warm Prospects/Website Analytics/World of Experience.

Framing UX Design Practice

Affect/AI/Artificial Intelligence/Atomic Design Methods/Big Data/Blackbox/Business/ CognitiveTaskAnalysis/Commonplace Book/Context/ContextofUse/Contextual-Activity Template/Copywriters/Dark Patterns/Data Capture/Deceptive Design/Delight/Design for User Experience/Design Methods/DesignSolutions/Design/Data/Capture/DesignCritique/ /DesignPractice/Digital Media/Effectiveness/Efficiency/Emotion/Engagement/Ethical Persuasion/ExpertReview/GenerativeInterface/Guidelines/HCI/Homecoming/Illustrators/ Interactive Installation/Lean UX Design Methods/Machine Learning/Minimal Viable Product/Muse/Odyssey/Online AB Testing/Online Funnel Testing/OnlineScaled-Up User Testing/Satisfaction/Shipping/Standards/SystemUsability/TabularTaskAnalysis/ TaskAnalysis/Technology/User Need/User Stakeholders/User Testing/UserRequirements/ UX Community/UX Evaluation/Work/Workflows/Worksystem.

UX Frameworks

AB Testing/Analytics/Banner Adverts Business Customer/Business Targets/Buy Now/ Confirmation Page/Conversion/Funnel/Conversion Rates/Design Problem/Design/ Solution/Design/Specifications/Digital Channel Information Architect/Join Us/ Optimisation/Personal Details Form/Product/Page/Prospective/Customer/Purchasing/ Journey/Quote/Page/Sales/Volume/Uptake/Uplift/Website/Website Analytics.

UX Approaches

AB Testing/Analytics/Atomic Design Methods/Banner Adverts/Best Practice/Business Customer/Business Targets/Buy Now/Buying Journey/Clarity/Confirmation Page/Consistency/ Conversion Funnel/Conversion Rates/Data Capture/Design Funnel Testing/Design Methods/Design Problem/Design Solution/Design Specifications/Digital Channel/Effectiveness/ Efficiency/Effort/Feedback/Flexibility/Generalisation Heuristics/Information Architect/

Join Us/Lean UX Methods/Marketing Journey/Minimal Viable Product/Optimisation/ Personal Details Form/Product Category/Product Page/Prospective Customer/Purchasing Journey/Quote Page/Rules of Engagement/Sales Volume Uptake/Satisfaction/Scaled Up User Testing/Technical Advances/Uplift/Upsell Journey/Usability/User Journey/ User-Centred Design/UX Analytic Tools/Website/Website Analytics.

UX Methods

Best-Practice/Business Practices/Business Process Modelling Notation Cognitive Work Analysis/Common place Book/Context of Use/Customer Experience/Data Capture/Design Method/Design Problem/Design/Solution Digital Media/E-commerce/E-commerce Systems/Experience Design XD/Experience Fold/Guidelines/Happy Path Process/HCI Engineering Design Principles/HCI Engineering Design Problems/Lean UX Design Methods/ Minimum Viable Product (MVP)/Model/Notation/Online AB Testing/Online Scaled-up User testing/Patterns/Port Speed/Practice/Principles/Problems/Process Design Methods/ Product Data/Model/Recipients of Our Designs/Reporting Lines/Research/Single Ease Question/Standards/System Usability Scale/Task Analysis/Tool/Turnover/Usability Online Design Funnel Testing/User Requirements/UX Analytic Tools/Work.

UX Case Studies

Ad Hoc Testing/Asset/Bespoke Version Buy Page/Checkout/Configure Purchase/Buy Page/Customer Journey/Feedback/Heuristics/Landing Pages/Marketing Journey/National Model/National/Site/Next Button/Page/Page/Types/Prototype/Pages/Review/Participants/ Previous Button/Product Category Detail/Product Detail/Product Detail Page Product/ Filter/Product/Finder/Product/Specification/Products/Progress/Meter/Review Scenarios/ Search Engine Content/Search Landing Page/SEO Specialist/Sitemap Specific Landing Page/Tree Test/Upsell Journey/Usability Study/User Journey/Virtual Assistant/Virtual Assistant/Engagement.

Appendix 2 Review

The appendix presents the final UX description. The presentation of the descriptors is to support readers in applying the description to their own UX practice and UX research and in completing the exercise assignments.